M000078293

Everything We Needed to Know About Business We Learned Playing Music

From the Band Room to the Boardroom,
Business Leaders Advocating Music Education
as an Instrument of Their Success

CRAIG M. CORTELLO

Everything We Needed to Know About Business,
We Learned Playing Music
From the Band Room to the Boardroom,
Business Leaders Advocating Music Education
as an Instrument of Their Success

Craig M. Cortello

U.S. Copyright © 2009, Craig M. Cortello

All rights reserved. No part of this publication may be reproduced, distributed or transmitted in any form or by any means, including photocopying, recording, or other electronic or mechanical methods, without the prior written permission of the publisher, except in the case of brief quotations embodied in critical reviews and certain other non-commercial uses permitted by copyright law.

First printing August 2009

La Dolce Vita Publishing (a division of La Dolce Vita Enterprises)
Metairie, LA

Quantity discounts and custom printing available on bulk orders.

Editorial inquires should be directed via email to
bizmusic@LDV-Enterprises.com

Edited by: Dawn Josephson

Cover design and interior layout: www.TheBookProducer.com

Distributed to the book trade by AtlasBooks Distribution
www.AtlasBooksDistribution.com

Printed in the United States of America

ISBN 978-09789900-1-5

Author available for speaking engagements, media events, and academic gatherings. For more information, visit www.BusinessMusician.com.

DEDICATION

In the aftermath of Hurricane Katrina, those of us who are proud to call ourselves New Orleanians experienced upheaval, heartache, pain, frustration, and loss in varying degrees – a home, a neighborhood or neighbor, a job, a school, a favorite restaurant or local store, a way of life, or most tragically, a loved one.

Some of the greatest losses of both resources and humanity came at the expense of the New Orleans music community. Far too many performers, supporters, and advocates of the Crescent City's greatest asset were displaced or lost in the wake of one of the greatest tragedies this nation has ever experienced. One of those supporters and advocates, a talented and beloved New Orleans radio executive and music writer and my sister, Karen Cortello, was one of those casualties, far too early at the age of 42.

Yet the lasting legacy of this storm will be that of rebirth – a community that will not let the city, its unique culture and spirit, or its incredible musical heritage fade away.

Like many of my fellow citizens, I was forced to reassess my life and my priorities. A rededication to music, perhaps the most consistent source of joy that permeated my life and my memories, seemed in order – a personal rebirth of sorts. Sometimes the best way to cope with loss is to find a cause worth fighting for, such as music education.

This book is dedicated to all of those associated with the New Orleans music community who have perished, and to those who fight to keep the music alive.

And finally to my wife Kim and my son Michael. There's no greater gift that a loved one can give you than to support your dreams. I love you both dearly for supporting mine.

Craig Cortello and La Dolce Vita Publishing would like to thank the following organizations for their commitment of both resources and support to this book launch:

FENDER MUSIC FOUNDATION

At the heart of the Fender Music Foundation is a belief that music participation is an essential element in the fabric of an enduring society. Their mission is to have the benefits of making music available to everyone in the communities in which they serve, to promote its importance through education and media initiatives, and to provide financial and in-kind resources in collaboration with other organizations to achieve their common goal.

 The Fender Music Foundation was created to provide funding and resources for music programs across America so that kids and adults alike will have an opportunity to experience the joys of music. They also educate the public on the value of a musical education.

This independent 501(c)(3) organization awards grants in the form of musical instruments and equipment to music education programs across the country. Over the past few years, the foundation has awarded 124 grants to music classrooms, after-school music programs and music therapy programs. Through these organizations, the foundation has directly reached over 35,000 people, including thousands of at-risk youth, giving them the opportunity to make music.

For more information, visit www.fendermusicfoundation.org.

Personal note from the author:

The Fender Music Foundation passionately believes in the life-transforming nature of music and shares an extreme concern that fewer and fewer people are experiencing the joy of playing an instrument. They also believe that those conflicting realities make inaction with regard to this trend unacceptable. That's why I approached FMF as a promotional partner – it's their attitude of refusing to accept the status quo of diminishing music accessibility that must become prevalent among music enthusiasts. By awarding grants to a broad array of worthy organizations, they are making a direct impact by putting musical instruments in peoples' hands, and that impact can be assessed by the testimonials of those recipients.

Their generous support and resources served as an essential catalyst in this book launch, and we are grateful and proud to have FMF as our promotional partner.

NAMM

Founded in 1901, NAMM (the National Association of Music Merchants) has been the engine driving the musical instruments and products industry, a thriving worldwide community of thousands of deeply passionate, talented companies that make, buy and sell the instruments that allow millions of people to make music. With more than 9,000 Members in the United States and 100+ other countries, NAMM is ultimately dedicated to leading the industry and creating more music makers.

NAMM's programs and partnerships include a variety of organizations and corporations, including Disney, Drum Corps  International (DCI), the Boys and Girls Clubs of America, American Idol the Magazine, VH1 (Save The Music), Sesame Workshop (Music Works), Piano Guy (PBS Television) and the GRAMMY Foundation. Among its many outreach programs are "Wanna Play?," a national public education campaign to raise awareness about the many benefits of music making and inspire people of all ages and talent levels to become active music makers; Sesame Street Music Works, a joint initiative between NAMM and Sesame Workshop that focuses on young children and music making; the organization's "SupportMusic Advocacy Kit," an extraordinary tool that brings exciting music/brain research home to NAMM Members and their customers; FORTUNE Battle of the Corporate Bands, celebrating the garage bands of adult music makers; the Weekend Warriors program, designed to bring baby boomers back into active music making; and the New Horizons Band project, designed to engage the "over-50" segment of the population in music making activities. Since 2003, NAMM has participated in the Tournament of Roses Parade, reaching millions of viewers around the world with its message about the proven benefits of making music.

For more information, please visit www.namm.org

Brought to you by **NAMM**

In 2006, NAMM began a national public awareness campaign about the proven benefits of playing music called "Wanna Play?" Since that time, the organization has reached thousands of people of all ages connecting them to the fun and proven benefits of playing music.

For more information, please visit www.wannaplaymusic.com

Personal note from the author:

During my early discussions with Scott Robertson of NAMM, he cited the Gallup poll statistic that "85 percent of Americans who don't currently play an instrument wish they had learned to play one." Truly amazing! I sensed their steadfast commitment to converting those non-musicians, and I am delighted that they've acknowledged the potential of this book project in facilitating those efforts.

NAMM provides the industry with critical research that gives an understanding of industry trends and supports advocacy efforts. Yet it's not simply the data, but their passion for music that shines through in all of their music advocacy efforts.

ADDITIONAL ACKNOWLEDGMENTS

To the 32 professionals who had such strong sentiments regarding the benefits of music education that they shared their time and thoughts generously. Their stories were both enlightening and inspiring.

Mom and dad for guitar lessons and for wanting a better life for me, and to 2 sisters who endured my playing.

The National Speakers Association New Orleans chapter and The Metairie Sunrise Rotary Club for their outstanding support, camaraderie, and commitment to serving others.

My publishing team, Dawn Josephson and Jim and Barb Weems.

Personal thanks to Moriah Harris-Rodger of The Fender Music Foundation and Scott Robertson of NAMM. Your commitment to and endorsement of this project gave this book launch momentum and credibility, and I can't express my appreciation enough. Thanks for everything that you do to promote the joy of music.

And to anyone who shines more light in the world through artistic expression and inspires others to discover their own voice.

CONTENTS

INTRODUCTION

A Conversation with a Jazz Legend

(The Marsalis "Music Battleship")

In the spring of 2007 I conducted an interview with Ellis
Marsalis, Jr. – best known as the father of the first family of
jazz in New Orleans and around the world – in preparation for a
Jazz Fest cover story I was writing for *Where Y'at* magazine, a
New Orleans entertainment publication. We sat in an office on
the second floor of Snug Harbor, the premier jazz club of New
Orleans located on Frenchman Street, just prior to the first set
of his regular Friday night show. The late George Brumat, the
former owner of the club, an avid supporter of jazz, and a friend
of the New Orleans music community, sat in the office with us
during portions of the interview. George was quick and eager to
comment on his friend: "He's the man who put this place on the
map. He's the franchise."

Ellis Marsalis's considerable accomplishments are sometimes
overshadowed by the fame of his sons Wynton, Branford,
Delfeayo, and Jason. Among jazz aficionados, however, Ellis is
considered one of the foremost jazz pianists and educators – a
true pioneer of the modern jazz genre. Some of the topics our
conversation migrated to were music education, the proper role
of parenting in a child's pursuit of excellence, and the role of the
arts in the development of well-rounded individuals.

"To me there's nothing wrong with somebody who has played a
musical instrument and is not going to do it for a living, choosing
instead to become the CEO of a major corporation, and there's

a ton of that," said Ellis. "I met a guy at Merrill Lynch who's a clarinet player. One of the best pianists we had, a young lady at NOCCA when I was teaching there – she's a banker in New Jersey" (NOCCA refers to the New Orleans Center for Creative Arts, an advanced program for young prodigies of music and the arts for high school-aged youths in New Orleans).

He indicated that his own understanding of the hardships of a musician led him to take a soft approach toward music with his children, though you could easily ascertain that he was an exemplary role model and a compelling force in his children's lives. "My view had to do with first understanding that being a professional musician is difficult enough without trying to make somebody do that."

So Ellis Marsalis, Jr. understood that regardless of whether the ultimate vocation of the students that came under his tutelage (including his children) turned out to be trumpet, saxophone, trombone, percussion, or banking and financial services, music education could comprise an integral component of their foundation for success. As he explained, it's only one element, but an important one in a well-rounded education that prepares a student for a diversified world and uncertain times.

"Music is sort of like a battleship," he said. "It's got every conceivable weapon on it that you can imagine, but if it runs into a fleet, it's in trouble. What we need to emphasize is to have a healthy fleet, not just one battleship...There needs to be mandated arts for graduation," he concluded.

On that note, let's explore the waters of music education.

1

Don't Start the Revolution without Me

(The Growing Respect for Right-Brain Thinking in a New Economy)

Former CEO of AOL Steve Case graduated from Williams College, a liberal arts college in Williamstown, MA. Here's an excerpt from his interview with the Academy of Achievement that offers an interesting perspective regarding the role that education played in preparing him for his career:

"Williams College is a classic liberal arts school, so there is nothing really business-oriented about it. There's no business classes. There's no marketing classes. I wouldn't say that any specific course really was instrumental. I do think that a general liberal arts education is very important, particularly in an uncertain changing world. I think what a liberal arts perspective gives you, is you know a little bit about a lot of things, and look at the world as sort of a mosaic and kind of see how the pieces come together. I think that gives you a perspective that I found to be very valuable.

"And so in one sense, there's nothing specific that I learned that was applicable. In another sense everything I learned was a useful foundation. Because I do think – not just in building AOL – but just the world in which we live is a very confusing, rapidly changing world where technology has accelerated.

"The pace of innovation has accelerated the speed of how companies react. I think the more you have a generalist perspective,

I think sometimes the more you can kind of see through the forest and the trees. And when it gets a little bit cloudy, you know, have some sense of, 'Well, maybe this might happen or maybe that might happen.' So I really am a big believer in liberal arts education. I think it's better – particularly in these kind of uncertain times – to know a little bit about a lot of things as opposed to being expert in one thing."[1]

Could we as a 21ˢᵗ century civilization be standing on a plane of intellectual shifting sands, one where creative thought, intellectual agility, and a comfort level with uncertainty offer the only island of sound footing? Perhaps this is just a backlash to the events of the last century. In the quest for mass production, prescriptive workplace procedures, and management systems that ensure predictability, we have paid a tremendous price. We have sacrificed individual freedom and slowed the collective evolution of business. It's an almost certain recipe for mediocrity in the new business world. We can apply a popular axiom used in corporate circles these days to the broader American economic quandary: "What was good enough to get you where you are today won't be good enough to get you where you need to go tomorrow."

John Kao is the author of *Jamming: The Art and Discipline of Business Creativity* and *Innovation Nation.* In the former book he discusses the effect that those prescriptive environments can have on employee morale:

"My desk runneth over with business plans from talented MBA students for whom a corner office with an impressive title just doesn't cut it. They don't want to work for big companies. They ply me for tips on how to escape corporate restrictions and tedium. MBAs are not alone in this. Many others entering to-

---

[1]   Academy of Achievement, *Stephen M. Case* (©1996-2008, http://achievement.org/autodoc/page/cas1int-3, rev. May 01, 2008)

day's workplace are emphatically unenthusiastic about sitting at a workstation, having to refer to an employee manual, and possibly losing their jobs when their employer decides how to downsize. They are learning the new truth about employment: that everyone today is his or her own entrepreneur and that the primary qualifications for this new role are imagination, inspiration, ingenuity, and initiative – in a word, creativity." [2]

In a workplace where employees are instructed what to do and how to do it with extreme specificity, the need and motivation for creative thought are diminished. When employee morale suffers, so does innovation. Employees who see the work environment as simply a place where you go to follow rules and do what you're told are rarely great sources of innovative inspiration.

Yet creativity and innovation are precisely the skills needed in a changing business environment. In the book *How to Think like Leonardo da Vinci,* author Michael J. Gelb echoes Kao's thoughts regarding the value of creative thought in a world of uncertainty. Gelb discusses the parallel between today's changing marketplace and the shift from the Middle Ages to the Renaissance period:

"It is safe to say that accelerating change and increasing complexity multiply the value of intellectual capital. The individual's ability to learn, adapt, and think, independently and creatively, is at a premium. During the Renaissance, individuals with a medieval mindset were left behind. Now, in the Information Age, medieval and industrial era thinkers are threatened with extinction. In five hundred years we've moved from a world where everything was certain and nothing changed to a world where nothing seems certain and everything changes." [3]

---

[2] John Kao, *Jamming: The Art and Discipline of Business Creativity* (New York: HarperBusiness, a division of HarperCollins Publishers, 1996)
[3] Michael J. Gelb, *How to Think Like Leonardo da Vinci* (New York: Bantam Dell, A division of Random House, 2004)

I believe there is a growing consensus that a period is emerging where a different set of skills will be necessary to succeed. So do we simply turn our liberal arts graduates loose in the boardrooms of corporate America? Perhaps that's overstating it a bit. The overall message is to work toward greater balance, or "whole-brained" thinking.

The Creativity Connection

Dean Deyo is a retired division president of Time-Warner who played music to work his way through college. He is currently the President of the Memphis Music Foundation and rekindles his passion for music occasionally in the classic rock band Legends of Rock. He expressed similar sentiments regarding "brain-balance."

"People are looking for well-rounded people today," he said. "When I was with Time-Warner, we were a big supporter of VH-1 *Save the Music*, and often got grants to bring musical instruments into the schools.

"I think with every business person, it would be nice if they had a little creativity. Maybe even if you didn't become the next Jimi Hendrix or Eric Clapton, a music education, hanging around music, being a part of the arts or entertainment and music – even the most logic-oriented person would get some burst of creativity from that. One of the things that I still find today is that just about every band that makes it – one of the reasons is because at least one person in the band has some general business instinct.

"The creative people need some of the traits that a good business person has, and a good business person needs some of the traits that a creative person has," he concluded.

In the book *A Whole New Mind: Why Right Brainers Will Rule the Future,* author Daniel H. Pink refers to the most current revolution as a transition from the Information Age that Gelb discussed to what he calls the Conceptual Age. He explains that the jobs occupied by the knowledge worker, a well-educated deployer of expertise and manipulator of information, are being outsourced or altogether eliminated by new technologies:

"Businesses are realizing that the only way to differentiate their goods and services in today's overstocked marketplace is to make their offerings physically beautiful and emotionally compelling. The high-concept abilities of an artist are often more valuable than the easily replicated skills of an entry-level business graduate. In the U.S., the number of graphic designers has increased tenfold in a decade; graphic designers outnumber chemical engineers by four to one. Corporate recruiters have begun visiting the top arts grad schools in search of talent. With more arts grads occupying key corporate positions, the rules have changed. The MFA is the new MBA."[4]

As Case, Kao, and Gelb did previously, Pink states the importance of creativity in the 21st century workplace, with concrete illustrations of the escalating demand for the competencies and sensitivities of the artist in the workplace.

Bridging Music to Business

So I came to research this book with a simple hypothesis – that music and the arts will play an increasingly prominent role in preparing our children for life and for success in the 21st century. As my research progressed, one thing became clear – the compilation of the body of evidence and analysis regarding the validity of my hypothesis was already well under way. I was boarding a train that had already left the station. But that's okay.

My task was to add to that growing body of evidence. I simply wanted to take the music slice of the arts pie, so to speak, and

---

[4] Daniel H. Pink, *A Whole New Mind: Why Right-Brainers Will Rule the Future* (New York: Riverhead Books, a registered trademark of Penguin Group (USA), Inc, 2006)

look for the attributes, lessons, and insights developed in music education to assess its value in determining business success.

In the best-selling business book *Good to Great,* author Jim Collins likens revolutionary change, in the context of the evolution of successful companies in this case, to the turning of a giant flywheel. He concludes that support for new ideas builds slowly at first and then accelerates until it's almost impossible to stop, as more and more employees lend their efforts and help push the idea forward.[5]

I have come to think of this body of work as another small push that will change the way we think of the role of arts education in determining success.

The flywheel is turning. Come along and push with me.

---

[5] Jim Collins, *Good to Great* (London, HarperCollins, 2001)

2

Pulling Out All of the Stops

(In the War to Save Music Education, We Need All of the Arrows in Our Quiver)

"In education, there is a connection between all of the pieces," said Michael Guillot, former Vice-President for Patron Services and Chief Advancement Officer for the North Carolina Symphony. We were spending some time together discussing the justification of funding for music and the arts. "Language, music, mathematics, and science are connected to our cognitive functioning. Any time I improve cognitive functioning in one place, odds are I'm going to get it in other places as well." As a former educator and elementary school principal, Michael is well-qualified and well-versed in this area.

And then he added the point that kept me grounded throughout the course of my research and kept it all in perspective. "But I've got to tell you," he added, "the other case we make is that in and of itself, art is worthy. If it had no effect on those others, it really wouldn't matter. It is a pursuit of quality of life, of personal joy, of meaning...And I don't want to get away from that."

Amen.

I have spent much of the last few years exploring the effect of music and music education on the development of skills, characteristics, and insights that contribute to business success. Yet I offer this text not in any way to suggest that music and the arts need such evidence to justify their existence. I simply understand that for those of us who have been fortunate enough to have been touched in a significant way by music education, music performance, and by mentors committed to sharing the joy of music with others, we understand that the effort to keep music education alive and well requires a Herculean effort, because failure is not an option.

Therefore, each additional bit of evidence to support the positive effects of music and music education builds momentum. In short, we need every arrow in the quiver.

3

Lessons of Hurricane Katrina, Thoughts of Renewal

(Let's Get it Right This Time)

On a sunny afternoon in May 2008 I was sitting in the kids' tent at the New Orleans Jazz & Heritage Festival. About a half dozen kids and their music instructor banged out rhythms on the drums while another half dozen danced to the beat. The children, their parents and friends, and the other audience members were all smiles. Beautiful artwork from area school children adorned the tent walls. They depicted happy images of New Orleans and its musical roots. The instructor spoke of our obligation to be a positive influence on our children, as he had obviously been on them. It was the kind of day and setting that gives you hope in what can be very cynical times.

The following day I watched an elementary school drama club version of *Willy Wonka and the Chocolate Factory*, with all of the foibles and mishaps that make school musical theater so charming. That experience only served to reinforce my renewed sense of optimism.

Then again, living in post-Katrina New Orleans brings with it persistent thoughts of renewal. Those of us who continue to call New Orleans home routinely contemplate the potential of a great American city to experience a transformation into an even greater community than that which existed before the storm.

What a unique opportunity we have to turn tragedy into triumph from the ground up. We have witnessed an influx of young professionals brimming with enthusiasm into the Crescent City, eager to take part in a civics lesson of historic proportions. Enrollment at New Orleans area universities is booming. There are great opportunities in front of us, but we have to get it right. The price of failure as our community and our nation attempt to address the issues of coastal erosion, flood protection, and emergency planning is simply too great.

As I write, with political sex scandals and corruption almost a regular nightly news feature, the ongoing war in Iraq, financial institutions and the general economy in peril, home foreclosures, etc., we can always use an uplifting experience every now and then.

And one thought struck me as I watched those kids perform: No matter how badly we screw up this civilization through war, addiction, violence, greed, intolerance, fear, bigotry, hubris, envy, or materialism, with every generation we get an opportunity to start over. Each child represents a renewal of sorts – a shot at redemption.

Mired in the ongoing process of raising an only child, I don't profess to know the magic formula of opening the eyes of our children to their potential and to the possibilities that this world presents to them. I only know that music is a part of that equation.

Like the Jazz Fest kids' tent performers and the drama club *Willy Wonka* cast, music has a unique ability to inspire us and to help us see the potential in ourselves and in others. Yet the temptation to minimize its significance with respect to prioritization of education funding is a real danger, especially in a community struggling to get back on its feet like New Orleans.

Let's not give in to that temptation. Let's get it right. The cost of failure in preparing our children for a rapidly changing world is too great.

4

Why Music?

(What Makes Music so Unique and Special?)

When the late, great Louis Armstrong was once asked to define jazz, he responded, "If you have to ask, you'll never know." I suppose there are things in this world we are not supposed to understand through definition, but rather through experience.

The logical question to ask before embarking on this quest to define music's magical power to develop our CEOs and business leaders of the future is, "Why music?" In other words, aren't there pursuits other than music education that allow people to develop skills, attributes, and insights that contribute to success in the boardroom? The answer: "Sure there are."

Yet I know that music is unique among those pursuits. We'll get into the supporting evidence throughout this book, but let's first look at the anecdotal evidence of the magic of music.

The Beat Goes On...and On

As we look at society, we quickly see that human beings just can't seem to be without music. We have home stereo systems. We have music in our cars. We have portable "boom boxes," but even those are becoming obsolete with the convenience of portable mp3 players.

Go to the gym and see how many people are working out to music. If we're not satisfied by the choices offered by conventional radio, we can listen to digital radio stations on our television or satellite radio stations. We step into the elevator or retail store and we hear music piped into the ceiling speakers. They even make waterproof radios for the shower. Think about it. We crave music so fiercely that we'll risk electrocution to get it!

Music is for every mood. During sporting events we play music beforehand and during the breaks to energize the fans. When we relax or meditate, we listen to mellow sounds. When we perform formal rituals such as weddings we play music, and we celebrate by dancing afterwards to music. At the other end of the spectrum, in New Orleans we have jazz funerals. We sing hymns to celebrate religion. We sing our children to sleep with a lullaby. Then we set the radio alarm so that the next day we can start the cycle all over again.

Music has an almost magical ability to touch both the hearts and minds of people. One reason is that it brings a familiarity that people find comforting. Because it is so pervasive in our lives, music is like a familiar friend or like a grandmother's quilt that's been in the family for years. We link nearly every defining moment of our lives spanning every emotion to a particular song.

For example, I hear Glenn Miller, and I'm watching old movies as a child with my dad...The Beatles – I'm nine years old and listening to my new Christmas present, the first album I've ever owned, *Abbey Road*.

I can listen to Boston's "Peace of Mind," and I'm back in my first garage band with the guys in 1980...Steely Dan – I'm spinning vinyl 33s on the family living room console turntable.

I hear the song "On Green Dolphin Street," and I'm watching my guitar hero Joe Pass perform live at the Varsity Theater in Baton Rouge...Boz Scaggs' "We're All Alone," – 1994 – I'm 29 and dancing with my wife at our wedding.

"Do You Know What It Means to Miss New Orleans" and I'm a Hurricane Katrina evacuee in 2005, waiting and wondering when I'll have the opportunity to get back home...Beethoven's "Ode to Joy," and I'm teaching my son to play a few notes on the piano.

Memories are often hazy. Linking those moments to music makes them so much more vivid.

Because music is such a strong memory retention device, it is also a powerful educational tool for children. The brilliance of Vince Guaraldi's musical accompaniments to the *Peanuts* cartoons that so aptly captured the essence of the characters of Charles Schultz is undeniable. His compositions were so revered and influential that music virtuosos such as Wynton and Ellis Marsalis, George Winston, Chick Corea, and B.B. King have cited their influence and paid tribute to them in song.

Music as Education

Decades ago, the late advertising executive David B. McCall lamented that his son could sing along with the songs of the Rolling Stones and Jimi Hendrix, but couldn't remember his multiplication tables. He gave jazz musician Bob Dorough the task of writing musical versions of the multiplication tables, and later expanded that concept to other subjects. Through Dorough's genius, the concept of *Schoolhouse Rock* came to life on Saturday mornings for generations of children who learned that "Three is a Magic Number" and that putting words and phrases together is easy at "Conjunction Junction" through short musical cartoon vignettes.

"Many school teachers adore me," said Bob when I interviewed him regarding the enduring popularity of the *Schoolhouse Rock* series. "Kids grew up with it, and they became teachers themselves. It's really a good educational tool."

So why is music so special? I'll just say that it is, and if you have to ask why, you'll never really know. But I suspect that you do already know it is special, not through definition, but through experience, whatever those experiences have been for you. However music has moved you and whatever emotions it has elicited from you, I suspect that you get it.

But perhaps you've never taken the time to examine how music has affected you, and specifically in ways it has helped you develop a foundation for success and for a more well-rounded and meaningful life. If those thoughts intrigue you, then perhaps this book will entertain, inform, and even inspire you.

5

Defining the Potential of Music Education in Business Success

(It's That 80-20 Rule Again)

There seems to be a great deal of evidence to support the hypothesis that music education improves math and science scores. That's a good thing. Remember what we said previously, "In the effort to keep music education alive and well, we need every arrow in the quiver."

It is true that students proficient in math and science are generally more highly compensated in the workplace. Yet that doesn't necessarily mean that math and science scores are the sole determinants of success, nor necessarily the most important ones. It's a basic principle of management that the importance of technical aptitude is diminished as a business leader moves up the corporate ladder.

I've worked most of my career in sales in engineering, consulting, and manufacturing firms, generally in the company of technically proficient professionals such as engineers, scientists, and mechanical design experts. Ask any of those professionals who have achieved a decent level of career advancement how much of their success they would attribute to technical proficiency, and the answer is generally about 15 to 25 percent. In other words, they can tie 75 to 85 percent of their success to other softer skills such as communication, leadership, teamwork, creativity, etc.

So the purpose of this book is to take a look beyond the effect that music education has on I.Q. scores and improvements in other subjects, to simply identify people who have been impacted by music education and have become successful in business endeavors, and to ask them to perform a little bit of introspective analysis. I asked these people to take a look at the business settings that they have found themselves in throughout their careers and to identify those skills, attributes, and lessons from their music education experience that were integral in their success. In other words, let's determine the impact of music and music education on that 75 to 85 percent piece of the success puzzle. I also discussed these concepts with music educators who have reflected on the impact of music and observed those changes in their students.

The chapters that follow are these people's stories, not a set of empirical data. There are volumes of scientific research written on the benefits of music education, and yet funding levels continue to fall. In fact, I use the word "research" only in the Merriam-Webster defined "collecting of information about a particular subject" use of the term.[6]

I have learned in my sales career that people often respond differently to compelling stories or testimonials than they do to facts and figures. Therefore, I asked questions of these professionals regarding their earliest memories of music, their influential music mentors, the music experiences that inspired them, the breakthrough moments when music ascended from a passing hobby to a defining expression of their individuality, and finally the parallels of those experiences that translated into success in the business world. I want you to *feel* their passion for music.

---

[6] research. (2009). In Merriam-Webster Online Dictionary. Retrieved February 22, 2009, from http://www.merriam-webster.com/dictionary/research

I want to elicit a more visceral and personal response. I can learn so much about the effect of music on someone's life when they vividly recall sitting around the family piano as a young child listening to their grandmother play as they sang along during the holidays, recalling the particulars of that setting in astonishing detail. I want you to feel the emotion of receiving that first guitar, getting that life-changing Beatles' album for Christmas, or playing that first live gig, because that's how music affects us.

And once we uncovered those stories to put each person's exposure to music in the proper context, I asked them to reflect on those experiences in an exercise of introspective analysis to connect the dots between music and business. There were several common questions that I asked almost all of the subjects, but I must admit that I gave them a great deal of latitude in our discussions. At times when the person simply wanted to talk about the general benefits of music education rather than specifically discussing the business correlation, that was okay too. If we're going to reap those benefits of music education that foster business success, we have to keep the programs alive with whatever combination of information will work.

These professionals are people who, like me, hold a common belief that music and music education transformed them in ways that are integral to their success, sharing their thoughts and emotions regarding that subject.

I've always had a suspicion that I developed into a better person – in every facet of my life including business – simply because I was exposed to music education, but it has always been difficult to articulate why. Over the years I've watched idly as music education funding has diminished, and I came to believe that my unique blend of business, music, and writing experience would provide a fresh perspective that could be beneficial to music educators. It became a story that I simply had to tell.

With each interview I completed, my joy, enthusiasm, and conviction skyrocketed. When you've latched onto your passion in life, it's amazing how the people around you provide support and resources to complete the missing pieces of the puzzle – a wonderful serendipitous series of connections leading me to the right people and leading them to me.

This book and the stories within and are fruits of that expedition. I hope you enjoy their stories as much as I have enjoyed listening to and compiling them.

6

Hail to the Educators

*(Through Sheer Will and Passion for
Their Profession, Our Teachers Consistently
Produce Wins in a "No-Win" Environment)*

God bless our teachers. It is staggering how important their jobs are yet how little society is willing to compensate their efforts. We demand accountability. Then when they produce standardized tests to demonstrate results, we chastise them for pumping kids with information and not teaching them to think. We live in a country where two working parents are the norm so we can adequately feed our insatiable appetites for consumerism, yet we fault the teachers for the lack of discipline in the classroom. We demand that our kids outperform the school down the street, yet we complain about the amount of homework that the kids bring home.

Teachers often spend their own money to fill the gaps in their under-funded classroom agendas. Administrators routinely look at budgetary shortfalls that are impossible to reconcile, and somehow they make it work. And they do it year after year after year.

There are many concerns with our formal education system, but given the demands and the challenges that our teachers face, characterizing them as anything less than heroic would be a tremendous slight.

So when I make my case for the funding and importance of music education, I don't make the case in an effort to tell teachers how to do their jobs. I offer these thoughts as a way to assist them in understanding the potential of music. Maybe a greater understanding of that potential will lead to breakthroughs in the way we integrate music into our curriculum. As Karen Nisenson, director of the not-for-profit group Arts for Healing (which uses music and art therapy to treat people with learning and developmental disabilities) attests, we are just starting to scratch the surface in the area of understanding the ability of music to help us reach our potential.

So let's keep scratching.

7

The 9 Parallels of Musicianship and Business

(The Keys to Success in Business and in Life)

So what are the magical qualities, lessons, and insights we can develop, learn, and gain through music and music education? We'll discuss these benefits of music education in detail in the later chapters, with stories and analysis from the lives of business and music experts, but here's the laundry list:

Confidence and Self-Esteem
(Stepping Up to the Mic)

One of the most common benefits of music the interviewees cited was the development of confidence and self-esteem. Consistently, I heard people speak of the positive effect that performing in front of an audience, mastering a new musical piece, or simply connecting with other musicians in an ensemble had on building their ability to believe in themselves.

Another quality directly related to self-esteem is the ability to handle rejection. Inherent with musicians and bands is the understanding that not everyone will like your brand of music or believe that you have talent. All musicians have a story about a gig where the venue, the equipment, the audience, or their own performance led to disaster. You just move on to the next gig. Also, auditions can test your belief in your abilities and your resolve. You emerge from those encounters with a thick skin.

Collaboration and Teamwork
(I'm in the Band)

A certain "give and take" comes from playing in a band where you have to assess the strengths, weaknesses, and personalities of your band mates. Fitting the complex pieces of that puzzle in a way that makes the music come together is quite an art. Those skills translate well to business endeavors or projects that involve teamwork and collaboration.

Leadership
(Conducting Your Symphony of Employees)

Applying the competencies of teamwork and collaboration takes on new meaning from the perspective of a leader. A conductor (or leader) must know the strengths of all of the musicians, understanding how their skills fit into the big picture of the orchestra. That conductor must then communicate a compelling vision, motivating the players to either step into the spotlight or to subjugate their own needs for the benefit of the whole, depending upon the circumstance.

Salesmanship and Branding
(Give the Fans What They Want)

Musicians and bands have to put together songs, performances, or identities that their fans (or potential fans) will find compelling. While greater musical proficiency will improve your chances of success, it's no guarantee. Repeatedly, participants spoke of how that constant campaign of engaging their fans and packaging their music in a way that creates loyalty served them well in business.

Creativity & Innovation
(Improvising from the Charts)

A common theme in all research regarding creativity is the "use it or lose it" theory. In other words, we all have the ability to be creative, but unless we think of creativity as a muscle that gets stronger with exercise or withers with inactivity, we'll never reach our creative potential. People involved in music come to the workplace with toned and fit creativity muscles.

Risk Acceptance
(Let's Just "Jam")

Before you can get to a place where creativity and innovation are possible, you must learn to trust the process that discards familiar, safe systems. You must walk out on that musical limb and have "jam" sessions – to just see what happens and assess the results afterwards. The people profiled understand that the greatest innovations often come when you leave the harbor of predictable outcomes and sail into the sea of uncertainty.

With musicians and artists in general, curiosity is strong enough to overcome that natural aversion to risk. The craving for a new sound or musical ideas overwhelms fear. Here's the proper analogy that characterizes the relationship between creativity, risk, and curiosity: risk anxiety is the brake that can halt the creativity train, but curiosity is the fuel that drives the locomotive.

For example, two children look into a dark cave. One child says it's too dangerous, and the other simply has to know what exhilarating mysteries lie within. In the world of jazz improvisation, the virtuoso lives for the next moment that takes a familiar song or arrangement into unfamiliar territory.

Discipline and Fundamentals
(Learning the "Scales" of Your Profession)

The discipline that musicians must possess to develop their craft to the point that they are even ready to share their talents on any significant level is often underappreciated. How many times had Joe Pass played a scale on the guitar, put chords and bass lines together in interesting combinations, or simply run through fingering techniques to stay sharp and limber? I don't know the answer, but when I hear his recordings, contemplating those questions is mind boggling.

Individuality
(Make Your Own Kind of Music)

Any form of expression, especially music, is an exercise in self-discovery. Determining what makes you unique is perhaps the most important aspect of personal development. Music and the arts help people find their unique "voice" in life rather than just going through the motions. There is perhaps no greater gift we can give our children than those tools of introspection.

Also, in the business world, differentiation is essential.

Passion
(Play it With Feeling)

Hand in hand with finding your unique talents is the discovery of your passions. We have too many people on the planet who are square pegs trying to fit into round holes. They have jobs and no purpose, a living but not a life, and they are avoiding the pursuits that they are uniquely qualified to offer to the world due to fear or complacency. Yet nothing great was ever achieved without passion.

The things I share with all the participants in this research are a passion for music and a belief that it is a powerful and inspirational force – the potential of which we are only beginning to realize. Finding that passion in music gives people an understanding of what you can achieve with it, and how any endeavor is destined for mediocrity without it.

8

The Participants
& Their Profiles

(It's All About the Stories)

The 32 profiles presented meet two important criteria. First, they have achieved a reasonable level of success by conventional standards. Second, they have been involved in music in some way and share a belief that it was a defining experience that contributed to their success in a significant way.

I talked with CEOs and other C-level executives, as well as small business owners. For a few, music is actually a part of their business. So for those individuals music has had a very direct impact on their business beyond those personal attributes, lessons, and insights that can be traced to their exposure to music.

I also talked to a few people who had backgrounds in education. It is alarming that as a society, we seem to have resigned ourselves to the reality that music and arts funding in education will continue to be diminished at a time in our history when the demand for innovation and creativity has never been greater. Those with experience in the academic world were able to share an insider's perspective on that subject.

I wanted to have geographic diversity, at least in terms of covering a sampling of people from across the United States. I was pleased that Andy Preston, a high-energy sales training expert from the U.K. and Neil Moore, a native of Australia now living in California and the founder and Executive Director of Simply Music, added their thoughts as well.

I also sought diversity in terms of the professions and industries of the participants. We have attorneys, non-profits, public relations firms, business telecommunications companies, a professional speaker, a restaurant business consultant, and an owner/manager of a fitness company. We have the Executive Producer of several hit television shows, a technology forecaster/business strategist and best-selling author, a regional administrator of the Environmental Protection Agency, and a veteran of several Silicon Valley companies that pioneered the introduction of computer graphics into film.

I must also point out that the participants achieved varying levels of accomplishment and success in their pursuit of music, and there were no minimum requirements. Neil Vineberg played guitar on Whitney Houston's blockbuster album in 1985. Traditional jazz clarinetist Dr. Michael White is the recent recipient of the prestigious National Endowment of the Arts' National Heritage Fellowship. And Bob Massie played jazz trombone in the Mel Gillespie Orchestra, a traveling dance band that played the Miss USA pageant annually and hosted parties for such jazz legends as Duke Ellington, Count Basie, Sarah Vaughn, Stan Kenton, and Gerry Mulligan.

Yet many of the business professionals simply play an instrument, participated in a garage band with friends during their adolescent years, or record music in the comfort of a home studio for their own pleasure. It isn't about their level of achievement in music; it's about the universal benefits of music they received that transcend music and foster success.

Skeptics might look at formal research into the benefits of music education as skewed data from arts educators justifying their existence. With the exception of a couple of subjects who are connected to arts funding, the majority of those profiled have nothing to gain from making this correlation and have no agenda here. They are simply conveying their thoughts regarding what music has meant to them and how it has affected the totality of who they are as a person, as a professional, and as a concerned citizen for anyone interested in this information.

There are two outcomes from someone reading this book that would give me satisfaction beyond words. One is that someone will be moved to action to either learn a musical instrument or to introduce an instrument into the life of a child. The other is that a music educator or education administrator will be able to justify the funding of a music education program or will be moved to take up that fight in some small part based on this information. I know how music can change lives because it has changed mine.

The 32 profiles are organized into three categories:

Business Profiles (18)
(Conventional Business Professionals with Unconventional Brilliance Resonating from Their Music Backgrounds)
In the first section of profiles, we gather the thoughts and experiences of a broad cross-section of professionals in a variety of careers/roles.

The Idea Factories (7)
(Business Leaders with Music Backgrounds Working in Creativity Fields)
Because of the growing demand for "right-brain" or creative, intuitive, holistic thinking in the 21st century workplace as previously discussed, I wanted to take a closer look at business environments that are traditionally considered creative enterprises. In section two we profiled professionals such as executives of branding and advertising agencies, public relations firms, marketing or consumer engagement organizations, and even the television industry. These experts provided invaluable insight into the correlation between music and the creativity needed in the workplace, and on the direction of the evolving business environment of the future.

Music and My Business (7)
(Professionals for Whom Music is a Part of Their Business)

I entered into this research with no intention of interviewing and profiling professional musicians. After all, there's no need to demonstrate the correlation between a music education and a career as a musician. Yet I came across several professionals for whom music is an integral part of their work who offered fresh perspectives on the role of music in fostering the tools for success – corporate keynote speakers/performers who integrate music with a business message, educators who have given careful thought of the role of music education in a child's development, and a music therapist offering insight into the ever-increasing recognition of the potential of music to transform lives. Section three captures the unique perspectives of professionals for whom music is an integral part of their work.

SECTION I

The Business Profiles

Conventional Business Professionals with Unconventional Brilliance Resonating from Their Music Backgrounds

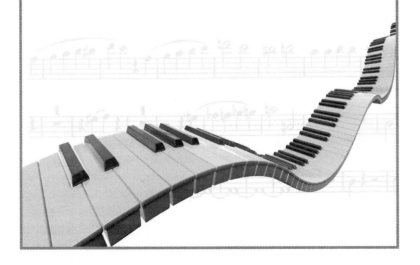

Dean Deyo, CEO & Drummer
**Retired Division President & CEO,
Time Warner Corporation
President, Memphis Music Foundation
Drummer, The Legends of Rock**

"The absolute terror of freshman in college for 90 percent of the population is public speaking. I never understood it because I had already been on a stage in front of thousands of people, and it was no big deal. For me communication, presence, poise, and confidence are all things that any good business person has to have."

* * *

"You've got to get to the point where you can make a presentation in a small room or make a presentation at a big gathering. Those performance skills that a musician would learn really translate well."

Dean Deyo had a successful career with Time Warner, serving most of his more than 25-year tenure based in Memphis as CEO & President of their Mid-South Division. After retiring and filling his time with various volunteer initiatives, the local economic development community tapped him to head up the Memphis Music Foundation. The foundation is sponsored by 22 of the largest corporations in Memphis, a list that includes FedEx, International Paper, AutoZone, and Pinnacle Airlines.

He is uniquely qualified to tackle this new challenge at the foundation, an organization that seeks ways to assist musicians in all aspects of the music business in order to drive the potential of music as an economic development force in the Memphis area. In addition to his corporate conquests, Dean is an accomplished drummer who paid his way through college playing music for the university circuit across the Midwest in the late 60s and early 70s. During that time, Dean and his band mates were called on to open for such well-known recording acts as Three Dog Night, Frankie Valli, The Buckinghams, and Question Mark and the Mysterians.

Dean grew up in the Chicago area. Like many other people, his earliest recollection of music was at the family piano. "We had a piano in our living room, and we had a tradition. Every Christmas Eve my grandmother, who lived with us, would sit at the piano and pound out the Christmas carols. We would all stand behind her and sing," he said.

Dean was required to take piano lessons, but decided an accordion would be easier to carry with him to school. "I decided quickly that pianos were fine, but accordions were cool. I had this red pearl accordion that was just gorgeous," he recalled.

In 1964 when Dean was 14 years old, his world forever changed. "It [the emergence of the Beatles] was out of the blue. It was just amazing. I can remember buying that first record, sitting there all night long and trying to figure out the song on the accordion. It took about three months of playing Beatles songs on the accordion before I figured out that there was no future in rock accordion," Dean realized.

If the emergence of the Beatles was influential, there was another particularly memorable musical moment that Dean experienced. He attended a concert that was every bit as vivid as the first time he walked up the catwalk at Wrigley Field.

"I can close my eyes and see every piece of it," he recalled. "I was in high school and I walked into the Aragon ballroom in Chicago. I took the train downtown. It was an old theater. I remember coming up the stairs, coming into the auditorium, the lights, this big velvet green curtain, and Jimi Hendrix pouring lighter fluid on his guitar and lighting it on fire. I can just see that in my eye. That was one of the first big concerts I had been to, and I remember walking away from that and going, 'Oh, my God. That was unbelievable. I want to do something like that.'

"I had some friends, and they had formed a little combo and had everything except a drummer. I said, 'Well that's me.' I always worked – I was a paperboy, a soda jerk, so I had money coming in. There was a drum set that I found at a pawn shop," he recalled fondly. "I went down to my dad and said, 'I've got enough money saved up, would you drive me to downtown Chicago, so I could buy my first drum set?'

"Music actually had some influence on where I went to college," Dean said. "We were playing pretty well in high school with a group of guys, and we were pretty much the same age. We left Northern Illinois University (NIU) every Friday afternoon after the last class. We played Friday and Saturday and were back on campus Sunday night raring to go."

Though Dean and his band achieved enough success to finance his college expenses, the nature of the music industry began to change as Dean began to pursue a career outside of music and settle down with his family.

"In college, every college campus had a ballroom," said Dean. "Some fraternity or sorority would rent the ballroom every weekend for a dance, and that's what we played. And it was great. When that kind of fizzled, we became a bar band. And we weren't a great bar band. Then disco hit, and that absolutely killed things. We weren't even close to that."

By then Dean was married, working in the cable industry in Rockford, IL. He still played in a little band. "We had a three bedroom apartment and my drums took up one of the rooms," he recalled. "I came home from work one night and my wife said, 'Honey, I found someone who wants to buy your drums.' We sold them for $250. I wish I had those drums today."

He didn't play again for 30 years. With a poignant gesture, Dean's wife set him back on the path to music after his retirement from Time Warner. "The year I retired from Time Warner, my wife bought me a drum set for Christmas, unbeknownst to me, because she had remembered selling them 30 years earlier."

He now plays in a band called the Legends of Rock with other boomers who have rekindled their love for classic rock.

"We're an unusual band," Dean explained. "We only want to play twice a month. Anything more is work. We ended up with six people who were just like us – had played in the old days, had all toured and recorded, some fairly famous. One was a doctor, one was a banker, one guy runs an audio company, and one lady writes commercials for radio.

"We play galas and corporate events," he added. "All we play is classic rock from 1965-72. We really enjoy it. It's sort of come full circle."

It is my observation that children exposed to music and the arts are much more advanced in their ability to be flexible and to adapt. What struck me about Dean's attitude toward working for a company like Time Warner during a period of rapid change was how he embraced that change rather than resisted it.

"For me, that [the evolving nature of the industry] was the only reason I was able to do the job for over 20 years," said Dean when I hinted that he must have seen incredible changes in the communications industry during his career. "Every six months we wanted to be something else. First we were a cable company. Then it was high speed data. Then we wanted to be a phone company. Then every six months we had something new we invented – analog to digital, pay-per-view, premium, OnDemand. It was always something new. That's the only reason I was able to do it that long."

Dean thrived in an atmosphere where others might have crumbled.

He also expressed the importance of presence, poise, and the ability to speak to audiences as a prerequisite for success – all traits and abilities that came relatively easily to him after performing in front of audiences during his music career.

"The absolute terror of freshman in college for 90 percent of the population is public speaking. I never understood it because I had already been on a stage in front of thousands of people, and it was no big deal. For me communication, presence, poise, and confidence are all things that any good business person has to have. You've got to get to the point where you can make a presentation in a small room or make a presentation at a big gathering. Those performance skills that a musician would learn really translate well."

Despite the fact that artists are not known for their ability to use "left-brain" (logical, analytical) skills, Dean was quick to point out that music requires a certain structure that is sometimes overlooked when assessing the positive influence of music on a child's development.

"Much of the stuff that I did in business, there was a model or a structure to it – sort of like songwriting," he explained. "When you're writing a song, there's a structure – an intro, a verse and a chorus, a bridge – and it has to be three minutes and fourteen seconds long if you want it on radio. If I was doing a PowerPoint or if you're building a resume, there is a structure that you have to follow."

There's also a work ethic lesson derived from his music experience that stayed with Dean throughout his career. "A good musician who is learning has to rehearse," he said. "They learn the value of practice."

Dean expressed the value of building relationships with other creative people at a young age and simply having something positive to funnel his energy. "Everybody in their adolescence needs something that they can grip on to," he said. "These were the people that I met with afternoons after school rehearsing. These were the people I spent my time with. These are the guys I hung with and became my friends. The same was true in college.

"It's friendships, but you learn teamwork," he added. "You are who you hang with. The good news is that musicians, regardless of some of the images they have occasionally, are generally a really good group of people. They have good ideas. They're creative. It certainly helped my development."

It only seems fitting that Dean now finds himself running a music foundation that requires him to draw upon both his business acumen and his understanding and love of music.

"It's [the funding of the music foundation] a realization from the business community of Memphis that music is important," he said with pride. "Every city today in order to attract the knowledge worker has to be a vibrant city. Nothing creates that vibe better than music. We are an economic development agency, and we are here to reinvigorate the music industry of Memphis." The Foundation provides business resources for local musicians such as computer access, training software, and databases of music industry resources, all free of charge.

Dean relishes his new role as President of the Memphis Music Foundation, indicating that it's one that he would probably have taken on for free, but he gets paid to do it. "I didn't see how life could be any better than that," he added.

Genevieve Thiers, CEO & Opera Singer

Founder/CEO Sittercity.com, America's
Leading Online Caregiver Matching Service
Executive Director, OperaModa
(Modern Opera Done Artistically)
Opera Singer

"Singers have to by nature sell themselves. They have to pre-package, market and sell themselves like a product. Naturally, every singer has all the skills to be an entrepreneur. When you're an entrepreneur, you see a niche and an opportunity in everything."

* * *

"Once you learn to channel energy and direct power when you're in front of people and you're singing, it's something you never forget."

Genevieve Thiers is the founder and CEO of Sittercity.com, America's leading online babysitting service. A babysitter herself, Thiers pitched Sittercity to Boston investors in 2001 and was told, "We don't fund babysitting clubs." Undaunted, she begged her father for $120 to buy the Sittercity.com domain and distributed 20,000 flyers throughout the city of Boston on foot, recruiting babysitters from local colleges while working a full time job at IBM and singing opera at night.

Five years later, Sittercity.com now has more than 500,000 users nationally including hundreds of thousands of sitters, and serves a huge cross-section of American parents with its online database. Genevieve was recognized by President Bush at the White House as the Small Business Administration Young Entrepreneur Champion of the Year for 2006, and she has done hundreds of appearances as a childcare expert on TV, radio, and in print outlets including multiple appearances on the *Today Show, Martha Stewart Living Radio,* the *CBS Early Show,* CNN, The *Wall Street Journal,* The *New York Times, Redbook, Parents, Parenting, Better Homes and Gardens,* and *Working Mother.*

The eldest of seven kids, Genevieve credits that experience for fostering her resourceful and creative nature. "We became extremely creative I think just to get attention," she chuckled. "It's been my biggest asset in business frankly."

At age 11 she began training in opera. Since then, babysitting and singing seem to have been the two constants throughout her life. She continued those passions while studying opera at Boston College, where she sang the lead for many of the shows and babysat to subsidize college expenses.

A twist of fate and of timing changed the course of her life. When she graduated from college, she wanted to pursue a Masters degree in opera. The female operatic voice generally matures at about the age of 30, so she needed to find something to keep her busy for a few years.

"I was staring out my window trying to figure out what I was going to do when I graduated, and I saw this nine-month pregnant mother walking up the steps from BC's lower campus to its upper campus posting flyers for a babysitter," she recalled whimsically. I said, "'That's interesting. That's something I can do in my free time. Why don't we take the model of an online dating service and apply it to child care?'

"When you're an entrepreneur, you see a niche and an opportunity in everything," she added.

Genevieve did eventually go back to get her Masters degree in opera from Northwestern, which she completed in 2004. Faced with the challenge of running a flourishing organization while pursuing a singing career, she once again summoned that entrepreneurial spirit and started her own non-profit opera company, OperaMODA (Modern Opera Done Artistically).

"When I graduated in 2004 I had this kind of dilemma where I thought, 'Okay, well I can't do what normal opera singers do,' which is go city by city all across the country and audition for apprenticeship programs," she said. "In fact I tried it. I made it to five cities, and then I missed a plane. I was sitting in the airport trying to figure out how I was going to handle this. I thought, 'The only thing to do is to start the opera company.' That's where OperaMODA came from, which is the opera non-profit that I run."

Genevieve has found that pursuing careers in music and in business simultaneously can be beneficial. "I can sometimes use one thing to leverage against the other," she explained. "So when things get really difficult in the opera world, I'll turn to work and really push that forward. And then the other way around. If work is getting really, really difficult, I'll go sing for a while, and it all gets a little easier. It's a leverage game. But if you use it right, you can make it easier."

Of course, there are only 24 hours in a day, and even someone with the passion and enthusiasm of Genevieve has limitations. She indicated that in 2004 she nearly drove herself to exhaustion. "I was singing lead in the show, producing the entire show, running Sittercity, and flying all over the country for that," she recalled. She learned that delegating many of the tasks associated with running the opera non-profit allowed her to find a more reasonable balance.

Genevieve recalled a few significant events that crystallized her enchantment with music. When she was eight years old, her aunt gave her a *Phantom of the Opera* tape. Genevieve says that she would sit in her room for hours playing the tape over and over, eventually learning the entire opera by heart. She would sing the entire show, excluding the male parts.

"Around the age of eleven, my mom put my sister and me in the local church," she added. "It was about a 2,000 person church, quite a large church. When we sang in front of the church it was the biggest occasion I'd ever sung in front of anyone. We really didn't have any idea what we were doing…we'd just throw all kinds of stuff in if we thought it would be interesting. We got this huge standing ovation. People didn't know what to make of it. They just thought it was the weirdest thing they'd ever seen. But apparently they thought it was cute or good or something. That kind of infected me. All performers have a moment like that, and they're off and running from there."

Genevieve also recalled an influential music teacher that helped her hone her skills, Mr. David Hall from Philadelphia, a high school music teacher. "He knew my family with seven kids had absolutely no money to speak of, so basically he taught me for free for four years of high school," she said. "He was the first person to take me under his wing."

"He was very patient," she said, revealing the essential characteristic that defined his excellence as a teacher. "When you first start singing, you don't know what you're doing. I was going in there trying to mimic Mariah Carey, and he said, 'Oh my gosh, you're hurting my ears, and that's not how you sing.' He pushed us just the right amount. He was firm when he needed to be."

I found it interesting in my research that people who had achieved so much success in business continued to essentially define themselves as musicians.

"First and foremost, I define myself as an opera singer," she revealed. "Entrepreneur is essentially a musical term. [Centuries ago] It was the name that was applied to a musical producer. The two of them are very linked. I wouldn't be anything like the way I am if I wasn't singing."

She added, "There's something really amazing about standing in front of an audience. You're giving them the song, and they give you a lot of energy back. Everybody's attention just focuses and sharpens. It's just this amazing moment. You're in front of everybody, but it's an incredibly private moment, too. There's a power that comes from that."

She went on to explain that once you learn to channel energy and direct power when you're in front of people and you're singing, it's something you never forget. You end up leading just because you're used to that energy transfer that comes from that sort of thing.

"You can't be a singer unless you are a leader," she said. "I've sung in front of audiences of 50, and I've sung in front of audiences of 15,000. You walk out in front of them and you have no choice. You must be the focal point of attention. You are going to lead them."

The early rejection that Genevieve experienced pitching Sittercity to investors didn't faze her. Once again, her musical training helped her to prepare for that rejection.

"In opera you have to have such a tough skin, because you go to one audition and they say you're amazing, and you go to a second and they'll tell you you're horrible," she said. "The problem is that your voice is inextricably linked to you. It is a horribly emotional thing.

"You end up with skin so thick that nothing scares you," she added. "You'll just walk up to anyone or start anything or make any phone call or go in front of anybody because you've got that strength behind you. You've been through the wash. It's really awful sometimes when it happens, but it makes you so much stronger."

That ability to dismiss rejection translates into salesmanship, according to Genevieve. "Singers have to by nature sell themselves," she concluded. "They have to pre-package, market and sell themselves like a product. Naturally, every singer has all the skills to be an entrepreneur. They've done it with themselves and their voice already. It's just expanding it out to a different product."

Genevieve echoed the comments of others regarding the discipline required to develop your musical abilities, and the application of that ability in business endeavors.

"Right now things are very intense with the company, because we are looking into a number of things that will really skyrocket our growth," she noted. "The rigorous discipline that you come up with in any kind of musician atmosphere translates very, very well into the real world."

Genevieve believes that music and the arts have the ability to reach students in a more profound manner than most any other subjects. "You can teach math, you can teach history, and you can teach engineering," she said. "They're going to learn a skill, and they're going to be able to utilize that skill at some point in their lives. But there are very few things that are transformative. When you're looking at academic subjects, they touch the mind. With singing and music, it touches souls. It's a completely different kind of communication. I do hate when somebody underestimates [the arts]."

Finally, Genevieve gave her perspective on her capacity for creativity, essentially an outcome of necessity, repetition, and desire.

"The only way to exercise creativity is to have so many challenges thrown at you that you have to work your way around them," she explained. "I realized how fast you get at problem solving when you're an executive of a web 2.0 company that's hurtling along at the speed of light. It [creativity] is like a muscle. You do have to exercise it. But the only way to exercise it is to make your self do something challenging. You have to want it."

James I. Palmer, Jr., Regional Administrator & Guitarist/Vocalist
Regional Administrator, Environmental Protection Agency Region IV
Former Guitarist/Vocalist, The Regulators

"I can say without any hesitation or doubt that my own personal musical odyssey has been a huge part of my personal and career development. When you actually get back from that investment [practicing music] every time you play, you build your own confidence knowing that you can do certain things and do them well. It has to be recognized in my own life and career in terms of relationships, confidence, leadership, and the feeling of belonging."

* * *

"As you look at my progression in my career, from MDEQ (Mississippi Department of Environmental Quality) to being selected by the President to be where I am right now, music has been a key part of the fabric of my own career."

James I. "Jimmy" Palmer is the Regional Administrator of the Environmental Protection Agency's Region IV and is responsible for a workforce of 1,200 people, managing agency programs over a ten state area in the southeastern U.S. He holds engineering and law degrees from Mississippi State University and the University of Mississippi respectively. During his tenure, EPA Region IV has been the leader in recruiting regulated entities into EPA's Performance Track program. Performance Track is an innovative initiative that fosters environmental excellence by encouraging regulated facilities to establish performance measures beyond those required by environmental law. Jimmy previously served in private law practice and in various capacities in Mississippi state government, including Executive Director of the Mississippi Department of Environmental Quality (MDEQ).

Music was never far from Jimmy during his childhood. His father grew up in what Jimmy referred to as "the red clay hills of east central Mississippi in the middle of nowhere." His father played guitar, fiddle, and French harp (harmonica), with the latter instrument accompanying him throughout World War II.

Jimmy's grandmother occasionally played piano, and he has many lasting memories of family trips to Biloxi on the Mississippi gulf coast. His own involvement in music was both a result of a strong music education program at his school and his father's love for music.

"My dad needed someone to accompany him on those instruments," Jimmy recalled. "The first thing he gave me, I must have been about four, was a little ukulele. It was one of those plastic ukuleles that had a device that you could clamp on the fretboard and punch the little buttons, and that would make chords."

When he was 10, he received his first guitar as a Christmas gift from his father. He played it so much that he literally wore it out and had to send it back for refretting. He kept the guitar until his senior year in high school.

"My dad taught me some very fundamental chords," he explained. "When he would play his fiddle or his French harp, then I was able to accompany him on the guitar. Coming from the hills of east Mississippi, he was playing old, old tunes that really go back into our country's folk era. The first song I learned to play accompanying him was 'Over the Waves.' It was very simple – three chords."

Jimmy later joined the school marching and stage bands, taking up clarinet and saxophone only because the band director instructed students to pursue the instruments that filled the bands' greatest needs.

Yet Jimmy's strongest early musical interest was singing, and guitar provided a perfect complement to accompany his vocal skills. "As I began to work toward my eighth grade years, the folk music scene really popped nationally," he said. "I was beginning to get into folk music. I bought a Peter, Paul, and Mary songbook and several others that I still have – The Beatles, The Kingston Trio, Hank Williams. Guitar really was the instrument I had the most personal interest in and the most fun with."

Jimmy sang in the school chorus too, and every year his chorale teacher would pick four boys to be part of the boys' quartet and six girls to be part of the girls' sextet. His teacher chose him to be part of the boys' quartet all four years in high school, singing baritone. During that time he asked one of the boys and one of the girls (the daughter of the chorus director) if they could sit down and sing folk music together. They agreed, and Jimmy made it work because he could play guitar.

In those early days of music, you can find the seeds of the leadership qualities that would later define Jimmy's career. "The choral director began to include us [Jimmy's folk group] in our concerts during the year. That was a singular thing in my memory – having that instrument and being able to anchor a group is very important. In the church choir I did the song leading. When I was chosen to be in the boys' quartet and then to be chosen to be the drum major of our high school band, those were leadership positions."

While there were music instructors along the way, Jimmy still points to his father as his primary music influence. "He was in my earliest childhood my strongest mentor on all of these instruments," he said. "In general, it was his love of music.

"As a teenager he acquired the nickname 'Shine,'" Jimmy confided. "I asked over the years several of my aunts and uncles about that, and I got a couple of variations on the answer. Two of them consistently said, 'In our teen years we would have barn dances, and your dad would always show out. He was going to play the instrument, and he was going to dance. So we started calling him Shine.' Until the day of his death, he was still known as Shine."

There was another life changing aspect of music for Jimmy that he shared joyfully. "I learned very quickly that being able to play guitar was something that the girls liked, especially when I put together that little folk group and later a garage band. I graduated from high school in 1965. I would carry my guitar over to Columbus, MS to the Mississippi State College for Women, now the Mississippi University for Women. A few times I would sit and play for Brenda, who has been my wife for 40 years. I've got pictures of myself that she took all those years back in high school of being out at Grenada Lake singing to her. That was a dimension of life I would not have had [without music]."

While Jimmy had exceptional qualifications that laid the foundation for his career ascent, his ability to foster relationships through music only enhanced his reputation as a leader.

"After law school, I was in private practice for three years and then went to the Attorney General's Office," he said. "That attorney general was then elected governor, so I went to the Governor's Office with him. I remember starting the second year of his tenure, and he wanted to have a Christmas observation event there in the Capital building in the rotunda. He came to me and said, 'I'd like to do something musical. What do you think?'

"I said, 'Governor, I'd bet we could find people here in the capitol building that can sing. He said, 'I'll just leave it to you. You put it together.' We sent out a general invitation to people who might have an interest in singing, and the response surprised everybody. I was the choral director. I remember so well setting up the bleachers in the rotunda. We then went to the governor's mansion, and he called the state orphanage and invited them to bring some kids to the governor's mansion for gifts and for singing."

When Jimmy came to the MDEQ, those positive memories of music from the Governor's office planted the seeds for his band, The Regulators.

"When I got to MDEQ, it must have been about year three, we were coming up on a once a year all hands meeting," Jimmy recalled. "I decided that I was going to poke fun at some of our senior managers by writing parodies using very commonly known songs. I sent out a general invitation to people that might want to play at this event, and they showed up at my door. It was ragged in the beginning. But by the time I had left MDEQ, we had tightened things down a good bit, these folks were talented, and I was glad to be able to just play in the group."

He then decided to get a group together strictly as an outreach initiative. "I wanted people to see environmental regulators in a different light; that we are human," he said. "We like to have fun. It all grew from there. We moved from parodies to real music. Number one: the band worked in a democratic fashion. We left our titles at the door. Number two: we were not going to play for any organization that was not a part of the regulated community. We turned down a lot of requests to come play a wedding or a party. I said, 'No, this is a state supported outreach effort. I'm not going to use state dollars for private purposes.' That's where The Regulators came from."

He proudly added, "It far exceeded anything that I thought we could do with the group. I saw quickly that we had talent there. It was a matter of getting it together."

Jimmy noted that the band was a great deal of fun and an escape from the environmental world. "We achieved that goal [public outreach] many times over," he noted. "Because on Monday morning, our folks were going to be sitting across the table from folks that we regulate, and we might have problems. So those relationships began to change for the better."

Jimmy reflected broadly on the role of music in his life and career. "I can say without any hesitation or doubt that my own personal musical odyssey has been a huge part of my personal and career development," he boldly proclaimed. "When you actually get back from that investment [practicing music] every time you play, you build your own confidence knowing that you can do certain things and do them well. It has to be recognized in my own life and career in terms of relationships, confidence, leadership, and the feeling of belonging.

"As you look at my progression in my career, from MDEQ to being selected by the President to be where I am right now, music has been a key part of the fabric of my own career."

Through music, children develop the confidence to lay themselves on the line, a trait that can be extrapolated to any pursuit. "Whether you become part of a high school band or your own group or what you do every day, you put your ego out there to be bruised, depending on how you perform or don't perform," Jimmy said. "You develop the self-confidence to be willing to lay it out there, subject to accolades or criticism, and sometimes both are what you need. I'm seeing myself standing up in the congregation in church leading the music. When you screw up while you're up there, everybody sees it."

All three of Jimmy's children grew up with music as a part of their lives, something that is a great source of pride for him. "Keeping a school music program in place gives an opportunity for kids to belong to a group where there's fraternity and collegiality," he said. "So many kids, and we see them tragically in situations in their later years, go off and do violent things. In just about every situation, somebody will say, 'Well he was always a loner. He never got along. He was not well liked.' Kids need to have or develop a sense of belonging that is very important in society in general."

As a young musician whose parents couldn't afford private music lessons, Jimmy learned the value of hard work and discipline at an early age. "There is a discipline that comes with anybody who is serious about playing an instrument. You have to just work at it. If you're going to play music and sing music at the same time, you've got to be disciplined."

Bob Massie, CEO & Trombonist
Founder & CEO, Marketing Informatics (Mi)
Former Trombonist, Mel Gillespie Orchestra

"There is no doubt that the way that I relate to my employees would be like a player/conductor. I'm on stage with them playing a role, but I'm also orchestrating what comes out of them. Years and years of practice and practice and practice – that refines the way human beings resonate with each other."

* * *

"It really affects the way that you get people to resonate in delivering great service to a customer."

Bob Massie is founder and CEO of Marketing Informatics, an Indianapolis-based company that specializes in direct marketing services. Founded in 1987, Marketing Informatics (Mi) boasts a comprehensive service offering for the direct marketing industry: market research, data analytics, creative and strategic services, data management, printing, and full-service direct mail.

The Kelley School of Business at Indiana University recognized Mi with the Entrepreneurial Award of Distinction in 2005 and 2006. Additionally, *Inc.* magazine named Mi one of the 500 Fastest Growing Private Companies in America on multiple occasions, achieving 1,100% growth during a three year period. Bob characterized it as the kind of growth spurt that is enough to "set your hair on fire," yet he seems to have managed it well.

He is also a published author, having written five books including one novel, and has served as author or editor of dozens of curriculum projects. His current project is a book entitled *Marketing is a Relationship.*

Yet for all of his success, Bob considers himself an "accidental businessman."

Deeply guided by his faith, Bob spent a dozen years in the ministry. He left to form a non-profit organization that provides education seminars on the culture and history of the Bible. He was unable to make the concept viable and was forced to take himself off the payroll and lay off staff to keep going.

With experience as a writer, Bob started farming himself out to do copywriting, mostly for fundraising organizations. That led to requests to handle the printing, then the mailing. He "blundered his way through" by his own admission until he had as much consulting work as he could handle. At that point he decided to make capital investments, purchase mailing equipment, and buy a printing company that he moved into his facility. Mi flourished from there.

Yet prior to his ministry work, Bob was a professional trombone player with a traveling dance band, and music consumed much of his childhood, adolescence, and early adulthood.

Bob's earliest memories include the church he grew up in, a small Baptist church in West Virginia with a very hearty bunch of music lovers. He also recalled fondly his mother's love of popular music, which included Bing Crosby, Perry Como, Percy Faith, and other crooners from the tail end of the Big Band era.

Perhaps the most prominent memory from his musical upbringing illustrates the effect that one music educator with a belief that music can impact lives can have on a community. The town in which Bob grew up shared a high school with a neighboring town. The music director, Charles Oshel, came out of the army in WWII. This was his first and only teaching gig.

"He just revolutionized the music education program in this tiny little town," Bob recalled. "It was a dominant force; this and the football team. If you had any passion, you went down one of those two tracks. A strong local music program – that was very important in the life of this small town.

"The band programs in the 1930s and 40s were very military oriented," Bob explained. "He [Oshel] came out of the military, and he was able to satisfy the old timer's need for the structured [John Philip] Sousa type of stuff. But he was one of the pioneers of injecting popular music into a band program. And interestingly for him, the popular music was the popular music that my mother loved at the time."

Bob began playing trombone in the fifth grade and always loved it. He recalled the watershed experience when he began to really take music seriously.

"The thing that flipped me over the edge – maybe 1966, I went to Morehead State University to the Cumberland Forest Music Camp one summer," he recalled with enthusiasm. "I played six or seven hours a day with kids that were better than me. All of a sudden, the world opened up and I thought 'Holy Criminy! I could lose myself in this.' I already had a love for it all, but that hooked me. I was maybe 15 or 16 years old."

Bob's following sentiments confirmed a recurring theme of many of the research participants – the concept that music can provide the link that keeps students who are not necessarily thriving or interested in the core curriculum from becoming disengaged with education.

"Music just completely filled my life," he stated. "That was life in the small town. I did school just because that's what you were expected to do, but I did it only as an obligation. Every waking moment I wanted to be involved in music someplace."

When Bob was a senior in high school, there was an old local traveling dance band named the Mel Gillespie Orchestra, part of the great tradition of the middle part of the 20th century. Mel picked up Bob as an alternate during his senior year of high school after football season. By the end of the year, he was their regular bass trombonist.

"That's the way I made my way through college," Bob recalled. "I had two or three really significant things occur related to that. The first one is we played east of the Mississippi, north to south. We played the Waldorf two or three times a year. We played the Miss USA pageant on national television in Miami every year. It was a great band. Mel was continually upgrading the material. It was a good jivin' group. It was the late 60s, early 70s, and it was the last hurrah of that kind of a group."

By the time Bob got into his freshman year of college, he had graduated to first trombone – the jazz trombone. He got every pick-up gig that came along and played Barnum & Bailey and Icecapades and everything that came into the area.

Bob explained that Mel was also the president of the local musicians union. "The other thing is that Marshall University in Huntington, WV, where I did most of my schooling, had an artist series," he added. "As the head of the union, Mel hosted parties for everybody who came through town. So I got a chance to go to parties with Duke Ellington, Count Basie, Sarah Vaughn, Stan Kenton. All of the big name players who were in their declining years, and they were the icons, or people like Gerry Mulligan, who were in their absolute prime. Getting elbow to elbow exposure to those folks in a quiet setting like that – it was just great. They were some of the best memories."

As the impact of religion manifested itself in Bob's life, the grind of playing music for the aging and often overindulgent crowd began to wear on him. He later completed a three year run near his home town as a school music instructor, which was a wonderful and rewarding experience. He led the band in the usual Friday night football game performance, but followed in the footsteps of his mentors by adding supplemental experiences to the music program. A vinyl band recording, a Disneyworld bicentennial celebration performance, and a production of *Bye Bye Birdie* were some of the memorable moments from his teaching experience.

I asked Bob to articulate the special qualities of a music instructor based on his experience from both sides of the equation.

"For me it was that they [his music instructors] cared about me. That got my attention, and that made me love what they loved. I don't think I consciously took that to teaching, but that's the way it worked out," he said. "I'm a people person anyway, and I just loved these kids. I loved being with them. I loved sharing their joy and their pride and their frustration in the experience of music. And I'm sure I passed along a lot of the thing that I loved to them because of the connection that we had there."

Bob's wife Dianna is also an educator and a musician. Collectively, they share the frustrations of an education system that is increasingly gravitating toward standardized testing rather than the total educational experience.

"Those principals that truly care about kids and the experiences that affect their lives will value music and the arts as highly as they value other extra-curricular or core curricular things," Bob said. "You're really looking at shaping a child's life, not just delivering some curriculum and standardized test. If you don't have a principal that has a concern for the child's life experience, it's hard to make a case. One of my wife's frustrations is that she has so little time on task because of things that the system puts in their day."

In terms of the crossover into business endeavors, Bob once again discussed the value of the musician's performance as preparation in becoming comfortable performing in a business setting.

"One of the reasons that I gravitated to the marketing arena is that I'm very comfortable being on stage. I like being in front of people. I'm in the direct mail marketing business. Pitching concepts, making presentations to people to help them understand and connect – there's no doubt that [music] performance gave me an edge up on others," he said emphatically.

Striking a chord with a team of employees is another dynamic where Bob draws on his musical background. "When you're dealing as a business owner or manager, you deal with people a lot," he explained. "There is no doubt that the way I relate to my employees would be like a player/conductor. I'm on stage with them playing a role, but I'm also orchestrating what comes out of them. Years and years of practice and practice and practice – that refines the way human beings resonate with each other. It really affects the way that you get people to resonate in delivering great service to a customer."

Bob also noted that the flexibility that comes from being a jazz musician capable of improvising provides benefits in the business world. "There's nothing like standing in front of an audience and having to deliver right out of your psyche," he said.

Bob's spiritual nature and his deep concern for others differentiate him from many other professionals, in terms of the way he connects with customers. He again pointed to music as a foundation in creating a more soulful side to his personality.

"The other thing is as a business owner, the life of my soul because of music is a little bit different in terms of what I connect with than my CEO peers," he explained. "They find interest and satisfaction and passion in things like sports. That's where most of it is, because you get guys coming out of sporting backgrounds who are very competitive and they tend to do very well in a business environment. It alienates me a little bit, because I'm not a very competitive guy.

"What it does for me as a business person in the life that I bring to this is different," he explained. "And I think in many ways it engenders trust and confidence among people, even though I can't banter about the latest golf score or whose batting average is this or that. There's a more visceral connection to folks."

H. Steven Sims, M.D., Doctor & Vocalist/Pianist/Trombonist/Bassoonist
Director, Chicago Institute for Voice Care
Assistant Professor, University of Illinois
at Chicago Medical Center
Vocalist, Pianist, Trombonist, & Bassoonist

"Courage is realizing your fear and going ahead and doing what you should do. So for me, realizing that I had stage fright, the confidence builder was that I did it. I was supposed to get up and do a solo, and I actually finished. That built the confidence. Something that I was terrified to do, I could prepare to do it and do it well, despite being afraid."

* * *

"As a surgeon there are lots of times when you make your incision, and it's a lot more challenging than you thought it would be... That experience helped me in terms of training me that when you get a little nervous, to use that energy to perfect your performance rather than fall apart."

H. Steven Sims, M.D., is the Director of the Chicago Institute for Voice Care and an Assistant Professor at the University of Illinois at Chicago Medical Center. He graduated from medical school and completed his residency at Yale University. He later completed a research fellowship at NIH on voice disorders and a clinical fellowship focusing on vocal cord surgery at Vanderbilt University.

Steve's chosen profession is a seamless extension of his passion, as he has been singing since the age of five. A talented and versatile musician, he started playing piano at age seven, trombone at the age of ten, and bassoon at the age of fourteen. He was nominated for McDonald's All-American band for trombone, and he considered going to college at West Virginia University on a band scholarship. "Then I got into Yale, and things changed," Steve said. As a "voice doctor" so to speak, Steve often has the unique joy of helping other singers recapture their health and return to performing.

One of Steve's earliest and most profound memories of music is of Ms. Betsy Thompson who sang at his church. "When I was four or five, she used to sing the song, 'If I Can Help Somebody' and 'Soon I Will Be Done with the Troubles of the World,'" he recalled. "I just remember being totally moved and captivated – totally in the moment of her voice."

Steve cited many of the Motown and Stax Records artists like Wilson Pickett, Gladys Knight & the Pips, Marvin Gaye, Johnnie Taylor, and Clarence Carter as influences, as well as others who demonstrated the intricacies of vocal harmony such as The Carpenters.

With music playing an integral role is his life from an early age, I asked Steve to envision what his life would have been without music. "I can't even imagine it," Steve stated emphatically. "I come from a musical family. My dad was one of thirteen, and I think all of his brothers and sisters sang. And my grandparents sang. Any time we had a family gathering, we sang around the table – Thanksgiving, Christmas, and Easter. At any of those large gatherings we had a lot of things going on."

He also sang with his cousins, he revealed. They would all get together and do concerts for the family.

Steve recalled a music mentor that played a significant role in his development, both musically and otherwise, Mr. Melton (Mel) Saunders. "I grew up in a small town in West Virginia," he explained. "He was the band director when I was in junior high school. Later, he took a job at the high school, and we moved together. He started with me in fifth grade, so I had him for seven years."

The defining characteristic of Mr. Saunders for Steve was his commitment to excellence. "We had these little cards – practice cards we used to call them," Steve said. "We had to fill it out every day – how long we had practiced. And we had to turn them in. Then he would have us play, and he would determine whether or not it sounded like we had practiced the amount of time we put down.

"And so it helped me develop a really regimented schedule to practice – 30 minutes on the trombone, 30 minutes on the bassoon, and then I would usually do 30-45 minutes on the piano a day," he added.

That structured approach to practice served Steve well in pursuing long-term goals such as a medical degree. "Putting the time in to get a result, having a vision, deciding what you want to do in life and laying out a plan – the practice really helped long term.

"He gave us structure, definitely," Steve said of his mentor. "It was always clear that he did not want people who did not practice. Those are the kinds of things that help with surgery. But I also think that band helps in different ways. It teaches you that you really have to be good at your part. It teaches you to learn how your part has to fit in with the other peoples' parts. You have to listen to what's going on and create a balance. Mastering that makes you better in whatever you do in life. Without it, there would be a difference in socialization, a difference in confidence, a difference in expression," Steve said of the many benefits that he has realized from music.

For some, the choice of vocation is a process that reveals itself gradually over time. For Steve, that discovery came in a much more abrupt manner.

"It [music] has always been a part of my life, but my senior year of high school is when I realized that it could be a career," he said with clarity. "That was when Annie Lennox had vocal cord surgery, and I became aware of that. At that time I was volunteering in the emergency room of our local hospital, and I was thinking about a career in medicine. I remember hearing on the news that she had some problem and had to have surgery on her vocal cords. I said, 'Oh, there's a surgery where you can operate on a singer.' That was my epiphany."

Music helped Steve overcome a sense of stage fright, an accomplishment that has reaped tremendous rewards, as a surgeon must be able to conquer those emotions and perform under pressure.

"Courage is not the absence of fear. Courage is realizing your fear and going ahead and doing what you should do," Steve explained. "So for me, realizing that I had stage fright, the confidence builder was that I did it, and I got to the end of my part. I was supposed to get up and do a solo, and I actually finished. That built the confidence. Something that I was terrified to do, I could prepare to do it and do it well, despite being afraid."

"As a surgeon there are lots of times when you make your incision, and it's a lot more challenging than you thought it would be," he said. "You have to maintain some degree of confidence and get through it. That experience helped me in terms of training me that when you get a little nervous, to use that energy to perfect my performance rather than fall apart."

Steve reflected upon moments from music in which he managed to perform well with minimal preparation and guidance by trusting his abilities. Again, the result of that experience is a confidence that transcends music.

"I sang on a worship team at a church I went to in Nashville," Steve said. "All of those people were professional musicians. On Sunday morning we would rehearse for 15 minutes before the service started. You got the starting key, a couple of chords, and a couple of words, and that was it."

That experience gave Steve a tremendous amount of confidence. He didn't know the song, so he had to listen, anticipate, follow the cues, and figure out how his part fit with two other singers and a band. It was a tremendous lesson.

"You have to train yourself to be sensitive to what other people are doing and listen in a musical group," Steve said of the teamwork dynamic. "That type of group activity is unique. And there are things about that – you have to be good at your part so that your part can fit into the whole. At the same time that you are being good at what you do, you have to be completely sensitive to everything going on around you so that the outcome can be its best.

"In terms of how I communicate in a university department, there are other people that I work with," he added. "You have to listen to what other people are doing and understand what they need so that you're not playing loudly when they're playing loudly – the balance. All of those wonderful things really help with interpersonal skills."

Steve also believes that music helps trigger the learning process for him. An auditory learner, Steve believes that listening to music helps stimulate his ability to acquire information. Even today, he almost always operates with music on because he believes it helps him focus and perform better.

There's certainly a sense of personal fulfillment that Steve finds in music, regardless of the supplemental benefits. "Even now, sitting down at the piano, playing something and singing something is complete catharsis. It's a way of making an emotional connection to the self. It's integral."

Steve's greatest sense of satisfaction, however, seems to come from the fact that he understands the importance of a healthy voice from his own musical experience. That understanding gives him a unique perspective and tremendous satisfaction, when he can come to the aid of his patients.

"To meet someone and within 15 minutes of meeting them, they're telling me their deepest fears and most private concessions to try to get at the problem that's bothering them," Steve conveyed. "It's marvelous to be able to say that I've trained and learned some things that can help you get back what it is you're missing. It's always the most wonderful thing for me when somebody comes back and says, 'It was so much trouble for me to try to communicate, and now I can do that easily.' That's a huge rush for me.

"Or when the singer comes in and says, 'I haven't hit a high C in years, and now I'm going up to D,' he added. "The excitement in their face. I'm right there with them cheering. To be able to help with that is a true gift for me. I'm just grateful and happy that my life worked out that way, because it truly is something I love. It's great to be able to share that with anyone who's having trouble with their voice."

Steve closed with a thought regarding the sense of well-roundedness that music and the arts afford participants. "Music in its own right is important culturally. Having that background in music helps you to present yourself as someone who understands lots of things about the world."

Sands McKinley, Attorney & Guitarist/Songwriter
Managing Partner, McKinley Irvin Law Firm
Guitarist, Songwriter

"I like to sit down and create a song. Using my imagination and creating something out of nothing enhanced and developed my intellectual and creative skills. My experience with music developed those creative and intellectual 'muscles.' I was able to use those muscles in different contexts as I got older."

* * *

"I created something out of nothing in my business life."

Sands McKinley is the managing partner at the Seattle-based family law firm McKinley Irvin. He and his partner and wife of 14 years, Rita Herrera Irvin, have built their firm to defy the unflattering negative stereotype of family law attorneys and to create a new benchmark for the practice of family law. The firm is the largest family law firm in the state of Washington, with offices in Bellevue and Tacoma.

Sands attributes his aptitude for creativity and innovation to a childhood and adolescence filled with music. While proficiency in those skills isn't generally thought of as a prerequisite for success in the highly technical field of law, the practice of family law is a bit of an anomaly. Given the number of variables involved, the personalities that come into play, and the highly charged emotional atmosphere that can cloud the judgment of the litigants, he considers every case a puzzle that requires a unique solution.

Stakeholders in family law cases are struggling to understand the changing social norms of the country and how current laws impact diverse populations such as gay and lesbian couples, unmarried couples with or without children, and elderly people that are divorcing.

"Today's family law system is much more complex than ever due to the increasing complexity of finances, relationships, globalization, reproductive rights, and the migratory nature of families," noted Sands. "These changes in societal norms are now issues in family law cases. It makes our work fascinating.

"What we do essentially is take people who are at the worst moment of their lives and in the worst emotional and mental shape that many of them will ever be in throughout their lives, with the exception of when they lose their loved ones," he added. "We have to work with them not just on a technical level but on a very personal level to get them through that process and have them come out of the other end in one piece and ready to move on with their lives. You have to have the right disposition for the work, that's for sure."

Sands recalled as a boy owning a toy plastic guitar that his mother gave him – a gift that followed him frequently. He also owned an old cassette player/recorder and would make up and record songs. At the age of eight he began guitar lessons. When he reached the requisite age, he played guitar in the stage band and studied saxophone, which he played in the school band through junior high and high school.

He also formed a rock band with friends in junior high and continued through high school. In college, Sands put his instruments aside during his freshman year, but soon began to feel the call of music once again. He purchased a four-track recorder, a drum machine, and additional instruments. He then spent much of his discretionary time recording music for his own enjoyment.

Law school and the early stages of his law career once again derailed his pursuit of music, but as was previously the case, that hiatus would be only temporary. Years later he re-established a studio setup in his home and bought new recording equipment. He describes his music as "Pink Foyd-esque" in the sense that there are intense combinations alternating between soft and hard passages.

For Sands, music has remained a constant in his life. He shared his thoughts on the instructors who planted the seeds of his affection for music from an early age, beginning with his first guitar teacher.

"She was very patient, very kind, and very encouraging," he recalled. "She was kind of like the difference between a parent who parents by earning and maintaining a child's respect as opposed to beating it into them. If I didn't practice during the week between my lessons, I worried that I would disappoint her. It made me really want to practice and stick to it at times when there are lots of things that can distract a young child."

He also recalled his school band instructor and saxophone teacher, whom he described as a "character managing chaos." Said Sands, "He was able to teach a band of 15 to 30 kids how to play our instruments. I look back at that now, and I think, 'Gosh that's talent.'"

While some music students have distinct moments that crystallize their affection for music, for Sands it was simply the experience of listening to great music.

"My mother was a big music listener," he recalled. "We had music on in the house all the time. She listened to a lot of Elvis Presley, Carole King's *Tapestry*, early Cat Stevens, and Johnny Mathis. I remember particularly with Carole King's music and some of Elvis Presley's music in his later years being almost hypnotized by the music. I would listen to the music on the stereo and pick apart the different parts of the musical composition – to separate things out and listen to how they were combined together, the different tempos and rhythms, and the lyrics, too.

"Not to sound corny, but it's almost a spiritual experience for me at times when I'm listening to music and hearing a piece that's very well done, either musically or lyrically, or most specially moved when those things are done well together. Early in my life it was a real intellectual and almost spiritual escape for me to lose myself in the music that I enjoyed listening to. Then later on when I was a teenager, I discovered Pink Floyd, and that was a religion."

First and foremost, Sands believes that the greatest benefit from music for him was the development of creative and innovative abilities, whether it was the primary force in that process or simply served as a catalyst in cultivating his innate abilities.

"Some of the characteristics that people would say about me now are that I'm an innovative person, a creative person, an entrepreneurial person," he said. "My interaction and involvement in music enhanced those natural tendencies of mine. The creative process is something I'm always engaged in, either in business or art. I draw a lot. I do architectural drafting, artistic drawing."

Sands revealed that as a child he had a lot of creative energy, and being able to escape into the world of music by playing and creating songs was like a "friend" to him.

"Some musicians are predominantly good at sitting down and reading music, playing music, learning it, and being extremely technically excellent at performing somebody else's music," Sands explained. "I don't enjoy that very much. I like to sit down and create a song. Using my imagination and creating something out of nothing enhanced and developed my intellectual and creative skills. My experience with music developed those creative and intellectual 'muscles.' I was able to use those muscles in different contexts as I got older."

And that experience had a direct application to his law practice. "I created something out of nothing in my business life," he added.

Sands sees music instruction as an integral part of a well-rounded, 21st century education. "First and foremost in my mind, music instruction will not appeal to every single child, but it's going to appeal to a significant percentage of those children, and in varying degrees," he surmised. "But even in the lesser degrees, being able to do it and appreciate it is a way to not completely cross over, but to "stick your little toe" into other dimensions in the universe that I can't fully explain. Because you can do that, it expands your perspective. It makes people better able to learn all of the other stuff."

Sands also commented that in order for the United States to stay ahead in the world economy, we have to compete on ever-elevated levels. That means we have to be innovative and creative people, and we have to develop young people who have finely tuned and honed intellectual and creative skills.

Sands joined the chorus of testimonials that substantiated the belief that the benefits of exposure to music and music education are far greater than the marginal improvements in I.Q. tests and math and science scores. He believes that the music experience fundamentally changes the way that a human being approaches every aspect of their life.

"It's part of the filter of the lens that you see the whole world through," he hypothesized. "So when you're seeing everything with an eye toward creativity, an eye toward innovation, and an eye toward creating something out of nothing, that's a far more relevant and practical reason to want to have music and art instruction in schools than trying to make people better in math."

Sands also pointed to the aspect of the discipline required for music education and the correlation with business. "The discipline and focus that you need to master an instrument – I definitely brought that to the practice of law as well as to the creation of the firm," he said. "I was always a perfectionist with music. I brought that same desire to optimize and bring the best to the practice of law and our firm. It required enormous amounts of drive and focus for extended periods of time."

But throughout the conversation, Sands continued to revert to the creative solutions required to address the complex problems that his clients encounter as the greatest applications of his creative abilities developed through music education.

"Our firm is all about, 'We're helping people,'" Sands said with pride. "We're creating solutions to problems. Every family is different, so every situation is different, and therefore every solution has to be different. We're working in extremely dynamic situations and coming up with ways to get our clients through those situations in a way that hopefully, at the end of the day, they're better off than when they first came in. They're ready to go on with their lives."

"It requires a great deal of empathy."

Andy Preston, Sales Trainer & Guitarist/Baritone Horn Player
Founder, Outstanding Results, Sales Training & Coaching Company, UK
Guitarist, Baritone Horn player

"Being in a band, particularly when you're on the road traveling, forces you to get along with people. That sets you up for business when you have a small team you're working with. You lean on each other, and that brings a lot more trust and rapport, a lot more honesty and truthfulness. But it also has an impact in a positive way on the results."

* * *

"I've always been passionate and enthusiastic, which is essential for having your own business, as I do now. And I was to a degree in my sales career. And that comes from having something to channel my passion and enthusiasm for, which was music."

Andy Preston is the founder of a highly acclaimed sales training and coaching company, Outstanding Results. Andy's firm provides help, guidance, and support to in-house sales teams of both large and small organizations throughout the UK and Europe.

With over 12 years of senior-level experience in the industry, Andy works with companies and their sales teams to improve sales efficiency and productivity. He regularly speaks at events and conferences throughout the UK and Europe and as a guest speaker at corporate events.

His client portfolio includes Bank of Ireland, Antal International, SQ Computer Personnel, Selecture Global, Evolution Recruitment and Be Resourcing.

Andy started off as a professional buyer. After watching less than impressive salespeople pitch their products and services, he decided to give sales a shot. After all, salespeople earned more money and got paid to talk to people…at least that's what Andy presumed.

As is often the case for first-timers entering the profession, Andy initially found sales daunting. "I found out after taking a telephone sales job quickly how hard it was," Andy recalled. But it was the challenge – or perhaps the desperation of survival – that turned things around for Andy.

"Just before the end of the probation period, my boss said to me, 'Look Andy, everybody likes you. The staff loves you. The clients love you. The problem is, you're not selling enough. So if we don't see an impact in the next couple of weeks, we're going to have to let you go.'"

From that point forward Andy was driven to succeed. His tireless work ethic and his penchant for differentiating himself from the competition facilitated his ascent to the top of his company and to the top of his profession in digital printed office supply sales.

Andy was later promoted to sales manager, a transition that while serendipitous, was not terribly pleasant. "I was a great salesperson. I was a hopeless sales manager," Andy admitted. "I got frustrated. I was stuck in a small office with no windows and computer printout reports. It drove me mental."

But Andy's transition into the world of sales management would provide the insight that led him to his current career. "I was then hiring in trainers and speakers to train my team, only to find out that the person who stood at the front doing the training had never been in sales," Andy said. "They had never picked up a phone in their life. And I thought, 'How can they train my team?' That's how I moved into the training and speaking world."

But music has been as integral a part of Andy's life as the sales profession. As a young baritone horn player, he played Manchester's esteemed Albert Hall. He later succumbed to the allure of rock music and migrated to the guitar. He toured the UK with professional bands, again conquering some of the large venues where he'd watched bands he'd admired as a youngster perform.

"I was musical as a kid," said Andy. "My parents bought me a drum kit, much to their chagrin I think. I was young, so I was bashing the hell out of it and broke a few of those."

Andy's first "proper" involvement with music occurred when he was eight years old. "My parents bought me a brass instrument – a baritone horn," he said, "I played in school, in the school band. I saw a lot of the UK and learned music to a fairly good standard."

Andy also recalled early family vacations, memories inextricably linked to music. "My parents had a holiday home over in Wales, about an hour and a half from my house," Andy remembered. "We used to make a lot of trips in the car. My parents always had one or two tapes they would play in the car back then – Lionel Richie, Billy Joel. It used to be like our holiday tape, so we used to sing along, clapping along.

"I was always as a kid, one of those annoying people who, especially when I was happy, would drive the teacher mad," he said sheepishly. "I used to bang on the desk and drum things, and generally get along. I was always around music, and music was in the house and in the car. I would take music off the radio and put my own mix tapes together."

There were moments in Andy's musical career when the gravity of his accomplishments came to light. "I played in a concert at the old Albert Hall, at the time the biggest concert hall in Manchester," he recalled with pride. "I was playing a baritone solo with the band, and had the sort of nerves you get before a big performance. There were probably a few thousand people there. I don't think it really hit me until that point, and I thought, 'I'd better take this seriously.'"

Andy again found himself playing sizable venues as a rock guitarist in his late teens and early twenties. "We were playing some big venues. I thought, 'I'm on a stage playing venues I've seen other bands playing, even some signed bands.' We were looked at for record contracts, but nothing ever really came off," Andy said of his success that approached yet didn't quite cross the chasm to fame and fortune. "I made the decision in my early to mid 20s that my career was going well, and that I needed to focus on that. Then music becomes a hobby."

The first thing that strikes you in speaking to Andy is his energy level, which undoubtedly serves him well in the sales profession. One of the certain advantages of his involvement in music was simply a constructive avenue to channel that considerable drive.

"It's almost hard to imagine it [my upbringing] without music, really," he said reflectively. "I was from quite an okay neighborhood. But had I not been doing music I probably would have gotten bored, sat in the park and drank, and got involved in small level gangs and that sort of thing.

"If you haven't got a focus, which music was for me, you can be messing around, causing trouble, and in trouble with the police. So the focus for me was music. It kept me out of trouble. It gave me a focus and a whole lot of pleasure throughout my life. Music brings so much joy to kids. It channels all of that adolescent energy in a positive way toward something meaningful."

Andy also draws from that ability to channel energy in running his business. "I've always been passionate and enthusiastic, which is essential for having your own business, as I do now," Andy stated emphatically. "And I was to a degree in my sales career. And that comes from having something to channel my passion and enthusiasm for, which was music."

Andy possesses a clear sense of self-confidence and poise, a necessity as a sales trainer and consultant. Again, Andy points to his musical roots and the accompanying stage presence for having established those qualities.

"Having performed, having played solos, and having been part of a band, it's almost like it takes all of the fear and nervousness away – particularly standing up and presenting in front of people or going around and doing sales meetings," he said. "You're so used to the anticipation and nerves and that kind of stuff from doing concerts, solo performances, and having been involved in music. It makes it a lot easier to do stuff that might have originally been daunting."

Touring with band members has provided Andy a new perspective on teamwork and collaboration, if not the ability to simply keep the peace with a potentially volatile mix of personalities.

"Being in a band, particularly when you're on the road traveling, forces you to get along with people," Andy disclosed. "It brings out that closeness. It's like living with five or six other people you can't get away from and forces you to adapt your own behavior to get along with people. In that close an environment, it's important to form a close bond with people."

It's that closeness that he believes set the stage for excelling at teamwork in business. "Whether it's your own business or it's someone else's, the bonds you get with those people are essential," he said. "The way I run my business, you've got people around you that you've got to support, and they've got to support you. You lean on each other, and that brings a lot more trust and rapport, a lot more honesty and truthfulness. But it also has an impact in a positive way on the results."

Resulting from a rich music education, Andy considers creativity one of his defining qualities. In a business world where differentiation is essential, that characteristic seems to serve Andy well.

"I still use music to channel my creative side," he said. "So I just sit and take a few minutes to rest, and possibly just put in some soft music to almost meditate, or some music that just puts me in that creative space that I enjoy. It puts me in the right frame of mind to think about what I want to achieve. And in business, I'm a huge fan of doing what other people don't do and being creative."

For example, Andy explained that in the UK, many people have stopped doing printed newsletters and send e-mail newsletters to clients instead. As a result, Andy is doing printed newsletters again so he can stand out.

"Particularly when it comes to sales, a lot of my background is in cold calling, and people have stopped cold calling. Great! So I get my guys doing it again and getting great results because they're prepared to do what others aren't prepared to. And that comes from being creative and differentiating," he said. "Certainly in the UK, and as I understand it in the U.S., there's a lot of pressure on price and getting deals done. If you can position yourself as different from other people, you're now able to get prices for what you offer and keep your profits up."

He added, "If you can get yourself positioned differently, which comes from creativity and the way you express yourself, you can win business even at a higher price."

Finally, Andy added one very direct benefit of music in the sales profession.

"If you're out doing sales calls and they aren't going well, all you need to do is put your favorite music on in the car – Van Halen's 'Jump' – anything that picks you up," he explained. "It's like you forget about what's going on. You're singing along to it. The ability of the music to pick you up from a time that hasn't gone so well is essential for a salesperson."

Monica Ricci, Professional Organizer & Drummer/Percussionist

Founder, Catalyst Organizing Solutions
Professional Organizer, Speaker, Author
Drummer & Percussionist

"I don't even like to think about that [growing up without music]. I can't even imagine what I would have done with my time during those years if I hadn't had marching band and drum and bugle corps. I really felt like I had no direction otherwise. What it gave to me was something to focus on, something to commit to, and it really pushed me to grow in ways I would have never been able to grow."

* * *

"It teaches you to be accountable to something other than yourself. It teaches you to commit. It's a great character builder."

Monica Ricci is a professional organizer and the founder of Catalyst Organizing Solutions. Her clients include GE Capital, Paramount Pictures, and the Environmental Protection Agency. She received the Founder's Award of the National Association of Professional Organizers (NAPO), and is also an author and professional speaker.

Monica is the author of *Organize Your Office in No Time* and is the former host of the weekly radio show *Organization Nation*.

When Monica started her organizing business 10 years ago, she wasn't sure it was a viable option to pursue. "It really came out of a realization that I wanted a business of my own, but I wanted a business that seemed like a natural extension of me," she said. "Organizing things and simplifying things was one common thread that seemed to run through my work life and my personal life. It was one of those things that I tended to just naturally do."

After pondering the idea for some time, she started to ask people if she could help them organize their spaces and things in their life. To her surprise, they said, 'Yes.' It never occurred to her that people would pay her to help them get rid of their stuff or organize it. That was the essence of the business.

"It was a thing I was just going to try, and ten years later it's my career," she said.

Monica also had a love for music as a young child. Later, marching band and drum and bugle corps became an integral part of her life. It's easy to understand how the precise and regimented routine of those experiences translates into success in her current profession.

"I remember being as young as five years old and sneaking into my mother's room to play her record albums," Monica recalled.

Monica indicated that her mother would often sing around the house, and she was heavily influenced by the music of her mother's liking. The Beatles, The Kingston Trio, and the soundtrack to *Jesus Christ Superstar* were some early musical selections that came to mind.

"I loved knowing the lyrics," she said. "I'm very into language and communication, and I'm a professional speaker as well. I have always been one of those people who could remember lyrics. Even as a kid, I would know the words to the songs on the radio. It's just something happy. I don't have a specific memory about any particular song or artist. I just remember always wanting the radio on. I would get in trouble at night because I would be listening to the radio in my room when I should be sleeping."

Monica even volunteered at a classical radio station as a teenager and received her broadcast license to be closer to music. And today, Monica said that she sings all the time in the house, even when there's not music on. It's something that simply makes her feel good.

"You can really connect with certain songs," she added. "Certain songs are inspiring and you feel like you can connect with exactly what they were thinking or saying when they wrote that song. Or maybe it's not what they were thinking, but whatever it is for you it has some sort of a good meaning.

"For me, music is just a powerful way to tap into what is really inside of you. There are so many songs I listen to specifically from artists like Jon Bon Jovi that talk about being fabulous – talk about being awesome and strong and powerful. It's really inspiring."

Although she always loved music, Monica never had any interest in being a musician, until the tenth grade when one of her girlfriends said, "Hey, why don't you join the marching band with me? It'll be fun."

"I think I played cymbals the first year," she explained. "I got really interested in percussion, and I learned to play the drums. The following year I played what were called triple drums at the time. I also at the same time joined my local drum and bugle corps, which was not affiliated with school. So I was doing marching band in the fall and winter, and then I was doing drum corps in winter, spring, and summer.

"It was just such an incredible time in my life for many reasons," she said emphatically. "It was one of the fondest times in my life that I look back on. Marching band was really fun, but drum corps was really more of a defining piece of my youth."

When Monica took up an instrument and joined the band and drum corps, music rose from a favorite pastime to an integral part of her life. "My band director, Mr. Rohrer, was somebody that I had a great respect for and appreciated," she recalled. "He was a little bit of a disciplinarian, but not tremendously so. And he really had a high standard. You could just tell that he wouldn't accept anything other than your best. He liked to have fun and we knew that, but at the same time he had a very high standard of performance. And his name is on the program, so one could expect that.

"He had a passion for music," she said, offering insight into the source of his excellence as a band director. "You could just tell. He was always excited, and he never seemed to be one of these teachers who are just putting in their time. He was always enthusiastic about the music program and specifically about the marching band. He really connected with the kids. That was what made you want to do well and create a great result. You didn't want to let him down."

Like many of the contributors to this book, Monica has a difficult time envisioning adolescence without music, given the tremendous time commitment she made to music during those years.

"I don't even like to think about that [growing up without music]. I can't even imagine what I would have done with my time during those years if I hadn't had marching band and drum and bugle corps," she contemplated. "I really felt like I had no direction otherwise. What it gave to me was something to focus on, something to commit to, and it really pushed me to grow in ways I would have never been able to grow. There are things now that I just know looking back over the years that drum corps had prepared me for. I'm so grateful for those years and to those people who committed time to those programs."

When asked to convey the benefits of music education specific to her experience and for children in general, Monica focused on the concept of teamwork, believing that music teaches kids about striving for excellence. Even when people think they are at their best, she believes they can always strive for better. "It teaches you accountability," she added. "There are very few things in a music program that have anything to do with the individual. It's a team sport. It teaches you to be accountable to something other than yourself. It teaches you to commit. It's a great character builder."

Monica also articulated the difference between the experience of marching band and that of drum and bugle corps.

"It's like the difference between college football and the NFL," she analogized. "It's like amateurs (marching band) versus almost professionals (drum and bugle corps). It's a lot more intense. The time commitment is huge. We would go into rehearsals in the wintertime and spend the entire winter indoors learning fundamentals. As soon as it got to be spring we we'd go outside and begin to learn drill. That carried on all the way through the summer and into September. It's a longer season.

"The rehearsals (drum and bugle corps) are 10-12 hours at a time," she said. "It takes all of your weekends. It's really a commitment for a young person to give up any shred of a social life. It becomes your social life."

Drum and bugle corps provided Monica a lesson in people skills not generally afforded adolescents. And that experience had a very direct application in her business pursuits.

"In the senior variety of drum corps you can be any age," she said. "When I was 15, I was marching with people who were 30,

35, 40, 45 years old. So I got to encounter people who I would have never met or have been hanging out with in a social circle. That's a very different experience than hanging out with 100 other kids who are all in high school."

One of the main lessons Monica learned was the sheer number of personality types in the world. She learned to approach different people in different ways. And because she marched with adults, she got to witness first hand how different people handle things based on their past experiences and personality.

"That's really helpful in business, because you can't treat every client the same," she said. "It also let me get to see how people react under stress. It can be very stressful. We're out in the summer, and it's 10 to 12 hour rehearsals in the heat of the sun. Some people get cranky, but other people don't. It's like a study. What can I learn from this person about maintaining calm in a stressful situation?"

Today, Monica attends a fair amount of networking events, many of which are structured meetings, and she believes that her past music experiences enable her to excel in these situations. "Being in drum corps taught me how to sit down, shut up, and let somebody else run the show and have the spotlight," she said. "And when it's your time for a solo, you'll get your solo. But it's not always about you. And that I think is a really fabulous lesson.

"I'm always shocked at how many adult business people in a business setting cannot keep their opinions to themselves until an appropriate time," she added. "The discipline that we learned in drum corps was that you're part of something bigger here. It's not about you. It's about the group, the team. If you do something stupid, you compromise the team and make yourself look bad. That's one of the best lessons I've learned."

She attributed those lessons of discipline and restraint to her drum corps instructor, Eric Kitchenman, whom she described as "the most intensely militant, driven instructor." Monica was fifteen or sixteen years old at the time. "He was so regimented and I just thrived under that," she said. "For whatever reason, it was just what I needed at that time. I learned a lot from him. Quite honestly, that's where I learned the term, 'Deal with it.' You don't get to cry about everything that doesn't go your way."

Such attributes as teamwork, commitment, accountability, and focus are what Monica credits to her music experience. "When you're in a music program, you have got to be able to focus your energy on what you're doing. You've got to discipline yourself. It's just mastery of your own body and your own space. Mentally focusing and being able to push through discomfort or inconvenience to get a good result."

Monica explained that there's a sense of identity found in musical expression that leads the musician to a place of comfort in one's individuality. "When you discover music or performance, it taps into your self-expression," she surmised. "You feel more able to express yourself, and you can connect with your soul on a deeper level." Such feelings often translate into confidence.

There's also a thickening of the skin that occurs in the pursuit of musical excellence. Because you have to learn to take direction and criticism and not take it personally, you learn lessons that most children never get to experience.

"As far as handling rejection, if you do have to audition for things, it's not personal," she added. "There were thousands of times when you're in a formation on the field, and you're moving from A to B. And for whatever reason, you're not in the right spot, and you're corrected. It's got nothing to do with you personally. It just means you're in the wrong spot."

Monica is keenly aware of the irony that such a team oriented experience had such real benefits on her development on a personal level. "The interesting paradox is that even though all of your training and discipline is about the group, each individual grows through the experience," she concluded. "And that's not about the group. Every person that I've talked to over the years who has spent any time in a music program, especially drum and bugle corps, because that's so intense, says 'Those were some of the best years of my life, because I was forced to grow.' Even though it's a great team thing, and it's all about the team, team, team, in the end it's the individuals who improve."

Dan Burrus, CEO/Technology Futurist & Guitarist
CEO & Founder, Burrus Research
Technology Forecaster, Best-Selling
Author of *Technotrends*
Guitarist

"One of the things that musicians and artists tend to do is explore other people's art and other people's way of doing things. I think we're looking for inspiration. I think we look at a level that non-musicians don't. Most non-musicians more easily stay in their rut."

* * *

"Musicians tend to find ways out of the rut, because that's what gives us joy – learning the new thing."

Dan Burrus is one of the world's leading technology forecasters and business strategists, and the author of six books, including the highly acclaimed *Technotrends*, which has been translated into over a dozen languages. He is the founder and CEO of Burrus Research, a research and consulting firm that monitors global advancements in technology driven trends to help clients better understand how technological, social, and business forces are converging.

The *New York Times* has referred to Dan as one of America's top three business "gurus" in the highest demand as a speaker. He has established a worldwide reputation for his exceptional record of predicting the future of technological change and its direct impact on the business world.

His client list includes many Fortune 500 companies such as GE, IBM, Oracle, Microsoft, DuPont, Yahoo!, Toshiba, American Express, Northwestern Mutual, ExxonMobil, and Sara Lee. He has appeared on programs such as Larry King, CNN, and Bloomberg, and is quoted in a variety of publications, including *USA Today*, *Fortune*, and *Industry Week*.

Over the years, Dan has founded five businesses, two in the experimental aircraft industry. Throughout his career, the constant has been his passion for all aspects of technology, including robotics, genetics, fiber optics, lasers, and artificial intelligence. He sums up the reason for his fascination with technology succinctly. "It lets you make the impossible possible," said Dan.

Yet Dan considers music an equally integral part of his identity. An accomplished guitarist who plays multiple instruments, Dan worked his way through college as a performing musician.

"The instrument was not an instrument – it was an extension of me," Dan explained. "The way I feel about the guitar is the same way I feel about my right hand. It's part of me. When I'm home, I play an instrument every day. I usually start out while the coffee's going by picking up one of my instruments and playing it."

I asked Dan if the motive for that routine is simply enjoyment or to initiate a mindset that facilitates the thought process beyond music. "It's a combination of those things," he said.

Perhaps there were early signs that music would play a prominent role in Dan's life. He was born in Portland, Oregon, and moved to Milwaukee, Wisconsin at about the age of two. He relayed the story his mother told regarding his transition to his new surroundings. "I was not a happy kid in Wisconsin until Mom happened to put on one of her records, which happened to be Hungarian Rhapsody No. 2. She started playing some of the music she had been playing in Portland, and I got all happy again."

Dan quickly tired of guitar lessons in the seventh grade, but returned to the instrument in high school and taught himself to play. By his sophomore year of high school, he was playing lead guitar in a band. While in college he continued playing in a popular college band, handling lead guitar and most of the ancillary aspects of performing, which was an experience that enhanced his business skills.

"I'm the guy who put the bands together," Dan explained. "I had to be an entrepreneur. I had to get musicians to come together, decide who's in and who's out – not unlike someone who's starting a company. I had to make sure that the skills were all compatible and worked together, and decide where we had to rehearse.

"We had to pick the right kinds of product – that is, songs that we wanted to play that people actually wanted to pay to hear," he added. "It's a tricky thing actually, because there are a lot of songs that musicians like to play that general audiences don't want to hear. That's actually customer demand and getting to know your customer, yet staying true to what's your core as well."

On the management side, Dan had to work with an agency that would book the bands. "I had to do contracts and paperwork, set fees, set prices, and work deals. I had to buy a van, get the transportation set up, hire and pay roadies, get the checks, and get the money disbursed. At the time I was not even thinking of it as, 'I'm a business guy.' Was it a training ground for becoming an entrepreneur? You'd better believe it," he said emphatically.

Dan explained that there are business lessons that can be learned by even those members who are not running the show. "There's working together as a team," Dan said. "There's playing, there's performing. There are so many parallels to running and leading a business. Those who weren't putting the band together had to learn how to not just show up, but to be part of a team and work together."

As one of the world's foremost advisors on technology and the accelerated pace of change, Dan offers compelling thoughts regarding the power of music as a creativity enhancement tool. "Innovation and creativity are the keys to advancing a society forward," he stated. "The only way that we can solve the problems that are in front of us is not with old thinking but new thinking, and learning how to think in an innovative, creative way is key to that. Tapping into the music side of the brain is a way to bridge the gap to the logical side of the brain as well."

Dan also offered for consideration the use of music or other interests of the student as catalysts in getting students engaged in education. Those sentiments have been expressed by many of the subjects of my research, and perhaps signal a need for a more flexible approach to learning that is tailored to the uniqueness of the individual.

"You want to teach lessons in a language they understand," Dan explained. "If you've got a boy who doesn't read or write very well and you try to teach him how to read a biology book, his eyes will probably glaze over. But if you give him a book on hot rods or motorcycles or something he's interested in, he might start to read that. What I want to do is play to their interests. And most kids are interested in music, but not all kids are good at school.

"So why don't we tap into their interests as a doorway to learn more about reading and writing and studies?" he asked. "Because that's where it leads."

Dan's words reminded me of my conversation with Ellis Marsalis, which I briefly described at the beginning of this book. What struck me about Ellis was a sense of a man who, at the age of 72, retains an infectious curiosity – an unending desire to continuously re-conceptualize his thoughts and philosophies based on his observations.

Those qualities give a sense of how he has instilled in his children an approach to music that is not simply an attempt to add a new twist to what their musical predecessors have achieved, but rather an impassioned quest to understand the nuances of all players, styles, and settings related to the jazz genre and beyond.

Dan provided some insightful comments regarding how that curiosity and awareness inherent in most musicians facilitates innovation.

"It's a cliché, but the only way to innovate is to get out of our own box," Dan said. "When I'm not growing, when I'm in a creative rut, there are things that can stimulate us to get out of our box and learn new things."

He used the musical analogy of Jimi Hendrix and the possibilities that his emergence in music opened up for guitarists. "He was doing things that I hadn't heard before, and that opened up a world to me to experiment in ways that I hadn't experimented before," Dan recalled.

"One of the things that musicians and artists tend to do is explore other people's art and other people's way of doing things as a source of inspiration," he offered insightfully. "I think we look at a level that non-musicians don't look. Most non-musicians more easily stay in their rut. Musicians tend to find ways out of the rut, because that's what gives us joy is learning the new thing."

Dan has given over 2,300 keynote speeches around the world. He attributes his comfort level in front of audiences as large as 14,000 to his music experience. "Even as a speaker and an author, I'm doing the same thing that I was doing when I was back in a band," he disclosed. "I'm on stage. I'm doing my gig. I think I was a shy kid at first. When you're on stage, that goes away. When people like what you're doing, you get acceptance."

We've previously mentioned the role of music and the arts in assisting young people in finding their true passions in life rather than just settling for a job or a living. Dan has clearly aligned his passions with his vocations throughout his career, a lesson he also attributes to music.

"I had a passion for the music," said Dan. "And every job I ever had I've had so much passion for that frankly, I don't even feel like I've ever had a job."

Dan also spoke to the rewards of practice in music, and the universality of that lesson. "The more time you put in, the better you're going to get. That's true with anything."

But once again, Dan believes that the greatest benefit of music is the simple joy and fulfillment that music has afforded him. "Music has been a big, big part of my life. I think the world itself would be a very dull place if music weren't in it. Music is part of all of us."

Lloyd Yavener, V.P. of Marketing, Underwriting & Claims & Drummer/Guitarist

Vice-President of Marketing, Underwriting, and Claims, Clements International
Drummer, On the Bus, Grateful Dead tribute band
Guitarist

"The insurance business is purely risk taking...You go in knowing there are going to be risks involved. Any time you play music, there are risks involved. You can have equipment failure. You can have rain. Somebody can get sick. Guitar strings break."

* * *

"Then there's the personal risk. There are going to be better people in the audience, and I'm going to be nervous. I'm going to forget my part. Or I've got to sing this really high part, and I hope that I can hit that note this late in the evening. There's a whole range of risk that you take in a band that's highly correlative to business."

Lloyd Yavener serves as Vice-President of Marketing, Underwriting, and Claims for Clements International, a leading provider of global insurance solutions for the Foreign Service and expatriate communities. Though not a practicing attorney, he is licensed in several jurisdictions, is a member of the Maryland State and District of Columbia bar associations, and has studied at The London School of Economics (General Legal Studies) and The University of Baltimore School of Law (Juris Doctorate).

Lloyd is also an accomplished drummer, with an extensive music resume as well. He currently performs with On the Bus, primarily a Grateful Dead tribute band in the Washington, D.C. area. The band has played everywhere from Capitol Hill events in Washington to University of Maryland block parties.

Lloyd played drums before he ever owned any. As a boy, he would stack up books to compile a simulated drum set. His older siblings were fans of the rock and roll hits of the sixties, and his earliest memories of music were simply being viscerally moved by the music of the day, including Bob Dylan.

"My sister had a Bob Dylan album called (The) Freewheelin' (Bob) Dylan," Lloyd recalled. "He didn't have the best voice. He didn't have the best playing ability, but there was something that came through, like a soul and an energy."

In the late 60s when Lloyd was roughly 10 years old, he migrated toward the heavier sounds of Jimi Hendrix and Led Zeppelin, combos that would profoundly influence his style of playing drums. "The first time I heard 'Whole Lotta Love' in '69 – after the kind of 'space' section where they came in with that big snare drum fill back into the song – to this day it brings goose bumps to me."

While in elementary school, Lloyd took violin lessons for one year, but he didn't quite catch on to the instrument. Then when he went to seventh grade junior high school, one of his classroom assignments was to assemble pieces or instruments within the room and make something out of it. Lloyd put together a drum set. "Of course, it was maracas, congas, castanets and all this stuff that wasn't rock and roll," said Lloyd, "but I arranged it like it was a drum set. The teacher said, 'You should really try out for the orchestra.' That got me my first introduction into playing drums."

Shortly thereafter, Lloyd was invited to a friend's house where there was a drum set, and he claimed that his dedication to drums and music simply took off from there.

He also provided some insight into the sense of dismay that is evoked in many parents when their children select drums as their instrument of choice.

"There was an old stereo that my parents had," Lloyd recalled. "They thought I needed to be institutionalized, but I piled the speakers up on books behind my head, behind my first drum set, and just cranked the music up. I'd just play along with the music. A lot of the stuff that I do today is maybe slightly non-traditional, but it works so well and becomes intuitive. The best music is when you're not thinking about playing – you're just playing."

While some drummers are seen simply as timekeepers, Lloyd views his role more broadly. "I've always thought of myself as a musician first and a drummer second," Lloyd explained. "A lot of the guys I've played with will comment on how dynamic I am. Of course, in a 'Dead' band we're doing jazz, rock, funk, blues, country, bluegrass – a whole range of music. I'm typically the one who will drive the real quiet dynamic passage in the middle of a jam. I'll sense the guitar player. I'm feeling what he's doing. Then I'll know that he's reaching the peak of his lead, and I'll pull way back on the drums."

Lloyd realized that he was hooked when he received his first drum set. "It was a 60s blue, sparkle set and not particularly high quality," he said fondly. "I got that set and set it up in my room for the first time. I had literally been playing on a drum pad and a couple of biology books as my set for one or two years prior to that. And then when I got this kit and started playing music – Jimi Hendrix, Deep Purple, The Allman Brothers – all these different styles of classic rock that were going on back in that day."

Lloyd began to explore new styles and expand his repertoire in college, where other musicians opened his eyes to jazz and syncopated rhythms. And to this day, he is still looking for people who can show him new stuff. He frequently watches "YouTube" to see people doing their solo drum clinics.

Lloyd narrowed his primary list of influences to two distinctive percussionists. "The people who influenced me the most as drummers – certainly John Bonham – the thunderous, heavy, straight-ahead rock and roll beat," Lloyd said with fervor. "It was not just the drums and the music. It was the heartbeat of Led Zeppelin. He was incredibly dynamic, hugely powerful, and had great 'chops.' But he never diluted those chops. Bonham had that super-huge, in-the-pocket powerful beat. Then when he brought his 'chops' out, it was like icing on the cake.

"The other guy was Richie Hayward from Little Feat," he added. "In college I really got into Little Feat, because he was doing so much of that syncopated and even a lot of Zydeco – those New Orleans rhythms that I hadn't heard as much. Those are the two drummers that to this day I still revere and study."

Lloyd also discussed the sense of wonder and joy that music injected into his childhood years. "Music should be a risk free environment," he said. "Unlike so many other things in life we do in business, family, and civic activities where there's caution and risk, music gave me the sense that this was a frontier – like you're one of the early settlers. The notion that there's this wide open frontier, the landscape's empty, and this is my chance to explore that wilderness."

Lloyd underscored my belief that the 'work' aspect of music is much more seductive than other educational pursuits, enticing children to work through challenging tasks to reach attainable goals.

"In school, homework was never fun," Lloyd said of his education experience. "Music for me was this thing that I could work so hard at, be so passionate about, put all of these hours in, and it was just cascading enjoyment. It just kept getting greater and greater."

Lloyd also referenced a recent study demonstrating that people will completely let their guard down and move to the beat of a song, a phenomenon of which there's no parallel in the animal kingdom or elsewhere in the human world.

"For me, it's (music) this sort of visceral feel that something's going on here," he explained. "It pulls you more than you have to run after it."

Lloyd also expressed his belief that music can facilitate a more interactive and enthusiastic learning atmosphere that infiltrates the entire education environment. "If you're putting books down, kids aren't going to naturally flock to the books and pick them up," he speculated. "If you put instruments down, kids are going to flock to them. There's this sort of natural attraction. Let them be free. Let them be creative. I think that would spill into other areas of education. Maybe they would get more out of it and be more enthusiastic about it.

"Music in many ways involves being interactive with other people," he added. "A good education environment involves an interactive environment where there's that experimentation, bouncing off of others, feedback, and reading other people. I think it's really helpful for kids to be open. And then when they're in the classroom, they're more likely to participate."

And Lloyd expressed the common theme of planting the seeds of self-confidence and presence through music education. "A lot of kids are afraid, especially when they get into adolescence, to get in front of a class. Nobody wants to give a speech or anything like that. The shyest kid, if he's got really good guitar chops, is not going to think twice about getting on stage in the talent show and letting it fly with music. I think music can help kids break down that barrier of feeling shy and not wanting to be in front of people."

Lloyd's realization of the synergistic dynamic of a music combo provided the necessary tools to bring together collaborative business teams. "In business, the Gestalt theory is critical. In an organization of any size, the whole has to be greater than the sum of its parts to be successful," he inferred. "Music has taught me the value of concerted action. We're not all doing our own things individually. That never works in a band. It has to come together. If there are dynamic parts, you all have to be together on that. If there are changes or breaks coming up, you all have to be reading each other. You can't have a successful band without that."

Even though Lloyd's band is somewhat of a hobby band compared to his day job, he and his band mates do spend a lot of time on that concerted action. As a team, they must determine their objectives, what they should do next, and what's important. When they're launching a song, they have to be together or it's not going to work. People often say that the best bands have 'chemistry.' Lloyd believes that's really just the shared objectives and the desire to work together.

"I've had a lot of success in business in that I'm not afraid to talk to people and say, 'We've all got to be on the same page here,'" he added. "And I did that in music without ever researching it and deciding that's what I had to do. You just come to the conclusion, 'Hey, you're playing at a different tempo,' or 'You're playing really loud and we're all playing really soft.' Developing that concerted action without the conductor tapping his baton and saying, 'everybody do this,' you learn that behavior of working together, having that shared objective and correcting each other openly when it's not working.

"It's been huge for my business success in terms of leading effective groups to bring that sense of unanimity and common purpose," he stated.

Lloyd also learned to accept and manage risk from his music upbringing, a trait that is absolutely essential in his line of business. "The insurance business is purely risk taking. You're insuring a cargo ship that's going overseas, and one in however many ships might go down. You kind of price that. You go in knowing there are going to be risks involved.

"Any time you play music, there are risks involved," he analogized. "You can have equipment failure. You can have rain, if you're outdoors. Somebody can get sick. Guitar strings break. There's just a range of things and circumstances that can create risk.

"Then there's the personal risk," he added. "There are going to be better people in the audience, and I'm going to be nervous. I'm going to forget my part. Or I've got to sing this really high part, and I hope that I can hit this note this late in the evening. There's this notion of risk in music that's inherent in business."

Lloyd uses what he learned about risk-taking musically in his professional career every day when determining calculated risks. "There's a direct correlation in business between how much risk you take and how much reward might be there. You don't want to go out there with your band and crash and burn because you're super-risky, so you're managing that to some degree – how many new songs you do, how aggressive you are with new material, who you bring into the band, and how much you stretch out in terms of good, large gigs."

Because music is inherently creative, musicians must have an open mind. And in business, if you're constantly doing the same things as everyone else, you're going to fall behind. Business requires that creative process that music brings out in people.

"The most successful people I know in business are not afraid to say, 'I don't know. That's interesting. Teach me something new,'" he added. "And the most successful musicians I know are always willing to listen to somebody else who's not even as good a musician. The old expression, 'A wise man can learn from a fool, and a fool can learn from no one,' is very true in music."

While creativity and discipline can be seen as opposing forces, Lloyd asserts that balancing those concepts can create a healthy dynamic in music and in business.

"To get good at something is to be disciplined," he explained. "Discipline is critical as you're breaking that new ground. There's a healthy conflict between discipline and creativity. You need both. It's that creative tension that's so critical."

And finally, Lloyd explained that there's really no substitute for a keen sense of enthusiasm in any endeavor, be it music, business, or otherwise. "It comes down to passion," he said, "When I see the people who are most successful in business, nobody is telling them to get excited about their work. They're excited about it just by waking up and being there. They're the best leaders, and they're the most positive."

Joe Santa Maria, V.P./G.M/
Owner & Guitarist/Singer
Vice-President/General Manager,
Fitness Management Systems
Guitarist, Singer/Songwriter

"Without that creative brain, you're not going to get great history teachers someday. You're not going to get great free-thinking politicians and great free-thinking urban designers. Those are the people musicians really are. That's where that funding should be considered."

* * *

"And that's what music does. It's just unfortunate that I feel music is looked at as an amenity to a high school rather than a true functioning piece of the curriculum. And how many voices aren't heard because it's not a real part of the curriculum?"

Joe Santa Maria is the Vice-President/General Manager of Fitness Management Systems in Worcester, Massachusetts. He started with the company in 1986 as a salesperson and worked his way up through the ranks into an ownership position. He is also a musician who plays a variety of instruments and was in the studio working on a CD when I spoke to him. His music could be described as Middle of the Road rock, straight ahead with a pop influence and catchy hooks.

Joe founded his own independent record company Ghost Sin Music, and his original music has been featured on Boston and Worcester, Massachusetts market radio stations, European compilation albums, and various Internet radio stations.

Guitar is Joe's primary instrument, though he had a rocky start in music. "My parents wanted to get me a little bit more discipline, so they got me guitar lessons from a very old guitar teacher," said Joe. "Of course, I hated guitar. I hated the lessons. There's no worse instrument to hand a child than a poorly built guitar. You're nine years old, you've got the softest little baby skin, and you've got all this barbed wire hanging about three inches off the neck [of the guitar]. I put that in the closet and decided to go back to baseball."

Like so many musicians, the Beatles were part of the revelation that brought music back into his life in a significant way.

"About three years later, my cousin gave me the crappiest cassette version of Sgt. Pepper [referring to the Beatles album *Sgt. Pepper's Lonely Hearts Club Band*]. I don't know what it was, but it was awesome – like an epiphany. So I found my guitar in the closet, and I was miming it into the mirror. Then I started poking at it."

From that moment on, Joe was obsessed with the guitar. "You're never seen without it, you're never photographed without it, you sleep with it, and you wake up and play for five seconds before you go to the bathroom. I don't have a room in my house since I was little that doesn't have a guitar in it.

"I can't even express the importance of [The Beatles]. Every band that I was ever in that I played with folks that appreciated the Beatles was a better band. There was something about picking apart the music note by note that you can do with the Beatles that you can't do with other groups because of the way they did things – the way they structured things," said Joe.

With boyish enthusiasm, he recalled the mystical joy of getting a new album as a child. "I can still remember that Christmas my mother got me the best gift in the world, *The White Album*," he said. "The double records and the posters and the pictures. I can still remember coming home from Christmas. I couldn't play the record. I got it, but then I couldn't play it [until he came home later that day]. I had to walk around with it all day."

He added, "Coming home Christmas night and crawling into bed and just looking at *The White Album!* Like 'I've got *The White Album!'* Looking at the lyrics and then just playing it really soft so no one could hear it. And to this day, it's still my favorite album of all time.

"That is missing from music now," he said in reference to the purchase of tangible vinyl as opposed to digital downloads. "I can't wait to see what the cover looks like, and I can't wait to flip it over and stare at it while I'm listening to it. The bands don't have that kind of allure to them. You had no money, so it was a big deal that you bought it. It was so much fun."

One of the funniest and most memorable anecdotes from my research comes from Joe's defining moment in music.

"The exact moment I realized that I wanted to be a whore for music? I was playing very, very bad guitar for the high school jazz band," he disclosed. "Five of us were asked to play Christmas songs in the auditorium for the school. We practiced all of these songs, and I didn't know how to play jazz guitar. I was up there, and I really wasn't playing half the time. I was doing a 'Stu Sutcliffe,' turning my back during rehearsals. The day of the performance, I showed up and my drummer was there. The jazz band decided that they were afraid to go out on stage.

"So here I am like 14 years old, with my $65 guitar," he chuckled. "I had an amp that must have been a hundred years old, like a big band orchestra guitar player's amp. I looked at the kid who played drums and said 'What do we do?' He said, 'Let's just go out.' We'll do 'Wipeout,' 'Smoke on the Water,' and we'll do 'Freebird.' It was southern rock with a little surf twist.

"The curtains literally opened up like in the movies. I'm sitting there with my little black T-shirt and my guitar, and it's absolutely quiet," he recalled fondly. "There's like 900 kids, and it's absolutely quiet. Mike just went into the 'Wipeout' opening with the drums. As soon as I started playing the guitar people went nuts, because I never made a peep [in school]. No one knew who I was. Then all of a sudden people went crazy, screaming and having fun. From that day on I knew – I've got to be connected [to music] in some form or another."

Joe discovered the power that music has to help students find a sense of who they are. "It gave me my identity. It gave me my voice in the world," he revealed. "It was my *thing*. Nobody could take it away from me. I had it to go home to. I could take it on vacation."

Music facilitated a sense of upheaval in his life that, although it created some friction, was a necessary journey of discovery. "All that stuff my mom and dad may have liked about the guy before the guitar and before music, it did go," he recalled. "The guitar brought with it rebellion and angst and anger, and other stuff they could have done without. It didn't exist before the guitar. That's what it does. It's bubbling up inside of you, and you just want to play that guitar 24 hours a day. You couldn't give a damn about anything else. As a youngster, playing that guitar was the most important thing in the world. I didn't study. I just figured I was going to be a rock star.

"There's something about youth that allows for free thinking. What were we rebelling against?" he asked introspectively. "Who knows? You just didn't want to be your dad. As much as you loved him, you didn't want to be your dad."

Looking back, Joe wouldn't change a thing. He believes that without music, he would have had a very different life. "The place where I was brought up was a very small town, and the people that I was surrounded by were very one-dimensional.

There was no diversity of culture. And I think without the guitar I may have slipped and been comfortable sort of working at the supermarket stocking shelves for the rest of my life or however it worked out."

So the outlet that was a source of dissonance ultimately served as a catalyst that allowed him to question the norms, providing a growth experience that changed him for the better.

"I don't regret that it caused so much disharmony in my home, because I think that was really, really necessary."

Joe offered his thoughts on the value of music education in terms of its ability to engage students outside of the mainstream. "I feel very passionate about this. Everybody cannot be a computer engineer. Everybody cannot be a lawyer. Everybody cannot be an accountant," he said. "The tendency is to slide toward the kids who are 'getting it' right away. They get it. They find the system, they work the system, and they get rewarded by the system – the honor societies and their picture in the yearbook. You know what, that's great. Those kids are working hard for that.

"We need masons, we need artists, and we need people to do advertising creatively," he explained. "We need all sorts of people that are the musicians. The musicians in your schools need support. And it's not about making them musicians for life. The reality of the situation is that they probably will play an instrument for the rest of their life more for enjoyment than anything else.

"But that creative brain is necessary," he added. "Without that creative brain, you're not going to get great history teachers someday. You're not going to get great free-thinking politicians and great free-thinking urban designers. Those are the people musicians really are. That's where that funding should be considered. It would just as well be considered in the math department for those kids who go on to be nuclear physicists. You're not teaching nuclear physics in high school; you're teaching basic math. But you put resources toward that in the hopes that they become nuclear physicists.

"And that's what music does. It's just unfortunate that I feel music is looked at as an amenity to a high school rather than a true functioning piece of the curriculum," he said with conviction. "And how many voices aren't heard because it's not a real part of the curriculum? America has a real tendency to really reward the typical. I have told school administrators that.

"Creative people just need a little pliability," he concluded. "If you can get them, you should hold on to them and put the effort into those folks. Find a way to have them apply the passion that they have for music and the freedom they feel from music into what you need them to do for a living."

Joe echoed the sentiments of others regarding the often overlooked ability of music education to instill discipline in the student.

"Music disciplines you in a very undisciplined way," he avowed. "To be a good musician you have to have focus. You have to have creativity and control of the creativity. I liken it to a garden hose that gets turned on. The hose goes flying all over the place. Sure it's providing water, but is it the most efficient way? As a musician you learn. When you're young you're hammering on that guitar making all sorts of noise. You're jumping around. When you get older, you realize I need to put 'A' in front of 'B' and then in front of 'C' and this is going to be a beautiful melody. And that's what I took to business."

Without his musical experience, Joe believes he would have floundered in business. He feels that that discipline of wanting to create good material is what made him a good business person. Additionally, the packaging and branding of the fruits of his creative labors fostered an understanding of those concepts beyond music.

"The fact that I nurtured a creative mind allowed me an opportunity to find a way to make money with it outside of music," he declared. "That has a lot to do with advertising and branding and design – things that have to do with making a company pop. If you have a company that offers a great product or a great service, but you don't really know how to tie it all together with a look and a feel and a smell and a taste and all that, it's not a great company. Without that music background, I never would have had the ability to do the branding and company organization that I have been able to do. That really made the difference."

Joe closed with his thoughts on finding a sense of self-confidence and an ability to believe in oneself, traits he once again traced to his musical roots.

"When it comes to writing music, I had a hell of a time until the day that I decided that I was just going to be myself," he said confidently. "When I was trying to write to a time or to a sound that I thought was popular on the radio or for a band that I was in, it was crap. All the music that matters that I've written has been the music that I've said 'I'm Joe Santa Maria. If people don't like it, they don't like it.' When I put stuff out there it's really me.

"It's the same thing with business. I just woke up one day, and I was working this job when I first started out. I was trying to do this and trying to do that. I said, 'I'm just going to be myself.' It's another huge cliché, but when you wake up and like the person you are, you're really much better off to everybody else than when you don't like yourself."

Dayna Steele, Entrepreneur & Rock DJ
Entrepreneur, Professional Speaker, Voiceover artist
Author, *Rock to the Top: What I Learned About Success From the World's Greatest Rock Stars*

"I like to use the analogy of driving a car. You can't learn to drive a car by reading a book or watching a DVD… It's the same thing when you walk out on stage, walk into an office, or you walk into a conference room."

* * *

"I can't give you a magic pill. You just have to do it over and over. You just have to walk in or walk on stage and do it… You eventually build that confidence."

Dayna Steele reigned as Houston's first lady of rock and roll for more than two decades, one of the most influential and respected radio disc jockeys in the nation. She played piano and guitar on and off for a number of years, but didn't pursue either seriously. Let's call Dayna's story "Success by Association." She had a front row seat to meet and greet the most enduring rock music acts of the last quarter of the 20th century including Van Halen, Stevie Ray Vaughn, The Rolling Stones, The Police, Motley Crue, KISS, and Aerosmith to name a few. Dayna was a witness to the traits that separate these superstars from one-hit wonders.

Dayna has carried those lessons forward as a successful entrepreneur. She founded and later sold the very successful Space Store, a successful retail and online space-related merchandise enterprise. She also founded SmartGirlsRock.com to encourage young girls to pursue careers in the fields of math, science, and technology. The website offers a line of T-shirts and products for teen girls designed to "make smart the new cool." She is a professional speaker, a voiceover artist, and an author. Gene Simmons of KISS wrote the foreword to her book, *Rock to the Top: What I Learned About Success From the World's Greatest Rock Stars*. One gets the sense when speaking to Dayna that the wheels are always turning, and that the next big idea is right around the corner.

Since many of the men in this book pursued music to impress the ladies, it's only fitting that Dayna entered the radio business to impress a guy.

"I literally got into radio on a dare in college," Dayna admitted. "I went off to college when I had just turned 17. Who knows what they want to be when they're 17? I must have changed my major and my living arrangements every semester. I ran into a local DJ – a big star – the biggest star I'd ever met. I really wanted to go out with him. He was making fun of the local radio station and dared some people to audition. I thought if I did that, he would think I was really cool and ask me out."

Dayna never did go out with him, but one thing is for sure... when she put on those headphones, she found her passion and her career for the next 22 years.

Dayna did enjoy the perks of the business. "That stuff was always fun – the hanging out with Sammy Hagar and Van Halen – walking into any restaurant in town, immediately getting seated, and rarely being given a bill. It was a fantasy land," she said.

But Dayna is also exasperated at times by the misperception that the life of a radio DJ is all backstage parties and limousines.

"One of the reasons that I wrote the book," she explained, "people would come up to me and say, 'Wow, you had such a cool job. What does it feel like now that you have to work for a living?' I would just look at them like they were crazy, because I worked 24/7 at being Dayna Steele. I volunteered for charities. I appeared everywhere. I read everything. I hung out with my listeners. I did everything I could to promote my business, which was being Dayna Steele.

"Another thing that spurred the book was people saying, 'I wish I was famous so I never have to work again.' These people work harder than anyone I've ever met," she said, referring to the frenzied life of a rock star.

Dayna has a very genuine "people" quality that seems to endear her to others, a trait that allowed her to outperform and outlast others in the radio business. She garnered a devoted following of listeners who came to be known as "Steeleworkers."

"I genuinely loved the music," she said passionately. "I wanted to do a quality product. I took care of the people who took care of me, and vice-versa. It's like that in any business. We called it schmoozing back then. I learned later it's called networking. I always say to people, 'What networking is first and foremost is just listening – just paying attention to what's going on around you and being aware of not only what people are saying to you, but what they're saying around you.'

"Second of all it's asking people, 'What do you want? What do you need? What can I do for you?' I met more musicians and more DJs who were always in it for themselves," she revealed. "And I found that when I did for others – when I found these new, up and coming bands and really went out of my way to help them, like Bon Jovi and Motley Crue, they remembered. They would come back and do my show. They would be the ones that would come back and give me the exclusive interview."

She then conveyed a story that vividly illustrated her selflessness and the "Karma-like" manner in which it has paid dividends.

"I love to tell the story of when David Crosby got out of prison here in Houston," she said. "He was doing exactly zero interviews. His agent was looking for help, finding him a doctor and a dentist and all those sorts of things. And nobody in town would help him, because they all wanted an interview. I immediately said, 'Well of course. This is my home town. I know everybody.' I got him hooked up. I understand he's not doing interviews. Maybe he'll do something with me in the future.

"Long story short, David and I got to be really good friends," she said proudly. "He did do a lot of interviews with me, and eventually he introduced me to the man I married (whom Dayna affectionately refers to as "Charlie the Wonder Husband"). So you never know how it's going to come back around."

Dayna has always loved helping people for no other reason than it's the right thing to do. And she's learned over the years that the more she does that, the more it eventually comes back.

Dayna observed that same sense of integrity from some of the musicians she met through the years.

"Sammy Hagar is not only a stand up guy and always a great interview, but he's always doing things for people," Dayna said. "I had a little friend here in Houston back in the 80s named Kevin who was 17 years old with Cystic Fibrosis. We had it all set up for him to go to the show with oxygen and medical personnel in case he needed it. That was when you could still smoke in the building, and that was devastating to Kevin's health.

"He got sick a couple of days before the show. Sammy and the guys, all of Van Halen got in the limo, went to the hospital, and spent an hour and a half in his room," she added. "It wasn't for VH-1, MTV, or *People* magazine. There were no media. There was no press release. Kevin died about two weeks after that, and I found out that Sammy had called him every day to see how he was doing."

And Sammy Hagar recently sold an 80 percent stake in his Cabo Wabo Tequila company for somewhere in the neighborhood of $80 million, evidence further illustrating Dayna's "give and you shall receive" philosophy.

Rock stars have a certain swagger, and it's Dayna's theory that it's simply a product of walking out on stage over and over again until the confidence becomes genuine. "I like to use the analogy of driving a car," Dayna explained. "You can't learn to drive a car by reading a book or watching a DVD. You can start and maybe get some ideas, but you actually have to get behind the wheel, start the car, and drive it. And when you think back to when you first learned to drive a car. That was the scariest thing in the world. And you hit curbs, you slammed on brakes, you made everyone around you nervous, and *you* were nervous.

"It's the same thing when you walk out on stage, walk into an office, or you walk into a conference room," she added. "I can't give you a magic pill. I can't give you a book. I can't give you a DVD that makes you go, 'Oh, that's how it works,' and you're going to go out there and be great. It's like driving a car.

"You just have to do it over and over, and you just have to walk in or walk on stage and do it," Dayna stated. "After you do it enough, after you drive the car enough, hopefully you get better. They [rock stars] were all nervous to begin with. You eventually build that confidence."

Dayna has an appreciation for the organization and attention to detail that is required of a touring rock and roll band and their team. She also discussed the concept of branding – how well enduring rock bands understand their fans and cater to those expectations. She shared a story from the band Van Halen that illustrated both of those points.

"Van Halen developed quite a reputation as rock star divas, because they demanded that the brown M&Ms be taken out of the bowl in the dressing room," she said. "And if they weren't taken out, the band would leave and go back to the hotel. They would not play, and they could still get full payment. Well, that's pretty devastating when you think of the hundreds of thousands of dollars that a promoter would have to shell out, and it did happen a couple of times. They developed this horrible reputation.

"The real reason they did it – Van Halen was one of the first bands to tour with seven semis full of equipment," she clarified. "And as you can imagine, the lighting, the stage, the equipment – if the specifications weren't met for weight and size, that could have been devastating. It could have hurt or killed the band. It could have hurt or killed fans in the audience.

"What the band learned is that if there were brown M&Ms in the bowl in the dressing room when they came for sound check, chances were either the promoter had just blown off specifications, or they hadn't even read the specifications," she added. "The band would leave, and the road manager, the stage manager and the promoter would go through that rider line item by line item. And more often than not, they would find that the truss hanging the lights or the stage weren't specified for that kind of weight. And that can be very, very dangerous.

"And then you get into good branding and marketing as the bad boy rock stars," she said of the effect of that perception. "They didn't do anything to really dispel the myth. Word got around to promoters they'd better follow that rider specifications to a 'T' or you're going to have problems," she said.

Dayna's latest passion is the speaking business, and her signature keynote topic is a motivational business speech entitled, *Find Your Inner Rock Star: Building Your Stage for Success.* Dayna concluded, "That same speech is good for seniors, incoming freshman, and *Fortune 500* CEOs. Rock music is universal."

Michael Guillot, Former V.P./Chief Advancement Officer & Guitarist/Vocalist

Former Vice-President for Patron Services & Chief Advancement Officer, North Carolina Symphony
Former Founding Principle, Virtual Development Group, Educator
Guitarist, Vocal Ensemble

"When you look at professional musicians or artists at any level, what you rarely see is the amount of time and energy it takes to get to that level of virtuosity. As a business person you begin to appreciate that. How many scales does Leo Kottke have to perfect to get to that level of excellence on the guitar? It's unthinkable."

* * *

"Yet that's indeed the journey in front of you. Every day you have to be willing to do a whole compendium of little things that all add up to greatness."

(Note/Update: Michael Guillot is currently pursuing a doctoral degree in Leadership and Change from Antioch University while working with a variety of nonprofit organizations in managing change.)

Michael Guillot recently served as the Vice-President for Patron Services and Chief Advancement Officer for the North Carolina Symphony. He is a Certified Fundraising Executive (CFRE) and has managed multi-million dollar fundraising efforts and activities for various organizations. He is also a former educator, having served as a teacher, a guidance counselor, and a principal.

For 18 years he ran his own business, the Virtual Development Group. In that firm he served as a business consultant, assisting organizations in developing their people and administering their fund raising programs. His client list included Boeing, Volunteers of America, the American Red Cross, United Way, Ronald McDonald House, and the Boy Scouts of America.

Michael's first prominent recollections of music were listening at church, recalling the real effort there to make music sound beautiful. When Michael was 12 years old, a family friend opened the door to music for him personally, and he responded.

"A friend of my father came home from an extensive work trip in Alaska, and he brought back a guitar," he recalled. "He gave it to me and said, 'I'm going to come back in six weeks and if you can learn how to play this song on this guitar in six weeks, I'll let you keep it.' And I did."

Like others of his generation, the music of the Beatles was hugely influential. He recalled the days when youngsters would hear songs on AM radio and make the trek to the drugstore to buy the vinyl 45s with the "A" and the "B" side.

"I would sit in front of the stereo listening to Beatles songs, trying to figure out what they were playing. I still listen to their music and think they are as powerful an influence on art in general as anything that's happened in the last 50 or 60 years," he said.

Being a part of that generation also opened his eyes to the power of music in terms of its potential for providing a conduit for social change.

"Art reflects life," said Michael. "It was expressing that era of heightened change, of personal discontent, of grappling with core issues, of looking around you and not making a connection between what you saw and what you felt. Some of that had to do with justice issues, of race. Some of it had to do with equity issues – how come so and so has this and other people don't? We claim to be the land of opportunity. Part of what we were striving for to identify in those days was how equitable was that opportunity.

"And of course, we were pressed on by a war," he added. "That war for me and many other Americans was not just an abstract exercise. We knew people who had lost their lives in that war and their families who had been affected. And of course I was at the age where I was eligible for the draft, so it was not an academic exercise.

"So to find any art form, but particularly one as accessible and as present as popular music to begin to tussle with those issues [was important]. At the same time you had the Beatles; Bob Dylan; Peter, Paul, and Mary; and Pete Seeger. You had the emergence of folk music becoming protest music, and popular music sort of echoing those themes. So Rock and Roll goes from just a mere expression of youthfulness to an expression of serious political and sociological issues," he observed. "It was a profound time. Many researchers call these periods golden periods, where a convergence of things happens. You look at Athens, you look at Rome, you look at the Renaissance, periods where art and civic and commerce and all these things come together. The 60s and all that it meant represented that time in the world. The first time the world had to stop and look at itself since WWII, and not necessarily liking what it found. You had a lot of art trying to tussle with that."

Michael's own involvement in music took a more serious turn as he moved from guitar player to vocalist.

"In high school I got involved in a superior vocal ensemble," he recalled. "We had a wonderful director who taught me how to read music, Malcolm Breda. He saw what we were doing, even though we were a small high school, as being at the highest level. He wanted us to see this as a pursuit of excellence.

"We rehearsed all day long, and it really became an important organization in my small school. He taught us how to read music and how to understand what the intent of the composer was. He introduced us not only to the fun music to sing, but also some challenging pieces. I really enjoyed the four years that I spent there."

Michael is well aware of the struggles of the education community to maintain funding for the arts, and he has strong ideas on that subject.

"As a former principal I would say that the right of the community to know whether schools are working or not is a fair expectation," he said. "I think it's fair whether you're a tuition paying parent or a tax paying citizen. Unfortunately, the current trend has been to emphasize standardized testing as a way to know that. I think that is a piece of the puzzle, but I don't think it's the whole puzzle, and I certainly don't think it's a big piece. Having been on the front lines and knowing that well, I would certainly be an advocate for abolishing the idea that testing can play such a prominent role in evaluating young people.

"So I think we have then sacrificed some things. I would tell you that I think that recess time is as important as other things for a child's development. The fact that we have taken those away because we don't have time for it anymore is really disturbing. I think physical, artistic development is imperative. I think in better school systems they still find a way to do that despite the pressure on testing, and I would hope that would continue. Because without that, I think we're going to grow an adult citizenry absent some of the things that make life worth living. I would regret if we lost that as a nation."

The North Carolina Symphony Orchestra is unique in that it was founded for the purpose of education. In its 76 year history this orchestra dedicated itself to serving the citizens of North Carolina by educating them. It has been playing concerts for fourth graders since the great depression, and it still does today. So education is part of the music.

When I asked Michael to articulate the takeaways of his experience with and observations of music that he now applies to business, his thoughts first returned to the vocal ensemble and of the lessons of his influential instructor, Mr. Breda.

"He saw that excellence and joy could be part of the same pursuit," he said. "That you could work hard, demand the best of yourself and the others you were with, and that would not diminish, it only enhanced your joy.

"That was an important lesson for me to learn. And I think it is [an important lesson] for young people where they tend to associate hard work with pain. I was taught that hard work meant that you could stand in front of a group of people and perform, and they would love you."

Having the opportunity to observe world class musicians up close has given him a greater understanding of and appreciation for their dedication to the little details that are considerable in aggregate.

"When you look at professional musicians or artists at any level, what you rarely see is the amount of time and energy it takes to get to that level of virtuosity. As a business person you begin to appreciate that. How many scales does Leo Kottke have to perfect to get to that level of excellence on the guitar? It's unthinkable. Yet that's indeed the journey in front of you. Every day you have to be willing to do a whole compendium of little things that all add up to greatness."

Michael has recenly had the opportunity to observe more direct music and business connections that have the potential to transform the workplace.

"To me, the power of music is that it transcends language. It is able to reach people without the necessity of language. Classical represents one genre of music, jazz perhaps another where the whole idea of words is not important – the idea that the sounds produced and the emotions generated by those sounds are shared. They're human. They're not bound by nations or political concerns. It brings people together in a way that if I had to use words, I'd lose the ability to do that.

"In business we often don't know how to celebrate. We don't know how to bring joy into our work. We tend to keep our nose to the grindstone, keep the flywheel spinning, all that other 'stuff, stuff, stuff,'" he said in a manner meant to convey the frantic and close-minded nature of the way we often approach our jobs. "I think we forget the humanity of this. The workforce of the future is going to be driven not by technology, but by people. I think bringing values and meaning to the workplace is the height of learning. If music can be a path to that, so be it."

Michael cites an example of Progress Energy, the large utility firm that is one of the symphony's largest sponsors. Occasionally the orchestra does a special concert for their employees. Two years ago Progress Energy employees and their families were invited to a concert, and many of them still talk about it today. That's the power of music's ability to bond people together.

"When business people want to bring that kind of emotional bonding, I think music can be a source of it," Michael concluded. "I want to create inside my workforce a sense of triumph over adversity. How many symphonic pieces have these stirring, rousing [movements] with just that theme embedded in them?

"One of the questions I always asked at the symphony was, 'How did you come to this music?' Why are you a regular symphony-goer? The number one predictor that I heard that's confirmed by research is that playing a musical instrument as a child was the reason that they continued to stay with music.

"That's the shame of what we're doing [cutting or eliminating music education programs]. By eliminating such programs in the schools, we're dooming another generation of never coming to this music."

Greg DiLeo, Attorney & Guitarist/Singer/Songwriter
Private Practice Attorney
Performing Singer/Songwriter, Guitarist

"The Beatles [tribute] show was a one-man show, basically undirected. That was a scary thought. The first time I played that, it was like the first time I tried a jury trial."

* * *

"Nobody's holding your hand, you're up there by yourself and you sink or swim. It's all on you."

Greg DiLeo is a sharp New Orleans attorney with a successful private practice. He gives brief bits of legal advice through his *Legal Minute* television spots. He is a member of the Louisiana Bar Association and stays active conducting pro bono work for various charitable organizations such as St. Vincent De Paul Society Conference and Ozanam Inn, a non-profit homeless shelter in the New Orleans area.

But Greg is also a talented musician. Greg's one-man show in New Orleans that pays tribute to the Beatles has received rave reviews. He plays guitar, sings Beatles songs, and tells the story of the Fab Four's New Orleans concert appearance in 1964.

The youngest of four siblings, Greg began playing guitar at the age of 11. He recalled the moment he made that decision vividly and the initial motivation behind his newfound passion.

"I started playing guitar because I was sitting in the living room watching a TV show called *Please Don't Eat the Daisies,* which was a TV version of a Doris Day movie about a *Brady Bunch* type scenario – a whole bunch of kids out of control," said Greg. "One of the kids, a little boy about my age was playing guitar, and he had a bunch of little adoring girls around him. I decided then and there that I wanted to learn how to play the guitar."

Greg's parents gave his siblings piano lessons, but none showed a particular affinity for music, so his parents didn't push music on him. When he came to them with the idea of playing guitar, they pointed him in the direction of an instructor in the neighborhood. Greg considered the music that the instructor taught to be very "square," and soon the student began to outpace the teacher, at least with respect to popular music.

"After a couple of years, I started figuring out songs on the radio, and the guitar teacher was copying my chords to teach to other students. So I quit," he said. He went back after a few years for additional sight reading training, but was largely self-taught.

In terms of the music that inspired and connected with him, Greg noted two distinct periods. "There were two very definite phases – the phase of top 40 at the time, which is what I started with," he said. "I've got this old music book where I'd write down the songs that I learned. The first two were 'Louie, Louie' and 'Wild Thing' because they are basically the same chords.

"The next phase was after I had quit my first round of studies, and I started learning Led Zeppelin, The Beatles, The Rolling Stones, and The Who," he added. "Every album and every single song on the album. When James Taylor came out I think I was 15, and I heard the *Sweet Baby James* album. And that's where I learned to finger pick. I got the music book and they had the tabs [guitar tablature] in the back. I was basically self-taught, and it changed the way I played."

That experience changed his preference from electric to acoustic guitar, and also kick-started his affinity for songwriting. "In the 60s, the guitar was king. When I could sing and play guitar at the same time, that was a breakthrough moment. I began thinking of the guitar as accompaniment for the voice," he explained.

As with so many musicians from the baby boomer generation, the Beatles changed the whole concept of music for Greg.

"They [The Beatles] were certainly musicians that made you want to identify with them. They were not just cool; they were trend-setters," he said. "They affected me to this day in that I don't like music unless it is melody oriented. If it doesn't have a melody, it seems worthless to me. The more I learn and play Beatles stuff, the more I appreciate how they influenced me in song structure.

"A lot of the songs told stories," said Greg. "Lennon wrote music as a vehicle for the words. He liked the way the words sounded together. It fits the music so perfectly that you couldn't think of any other words that could go better."

Greg also noted how the Beatles changed the rules of popular music. "It freed everybody to do whatever they wanted," he surmised. "The songs didn't have to be two minutes and 50 seconds anymore. You could make it longer if you wanted to. It's as long as it needs to be. Don't follow any rules. They always did something to make the song special."

Often, involvement in music profoundly impacts an adolescent's formative years. Greg described the effect that music had on him.

"I had friends, and even close friends. But when you're a teenager, you spend most of your nights alone," he confided. "I considered the guitar to be a friend. It was almost like a twin brother. I have these memories of just sitting on my bed, daydreaming, looking at my reflection in the back of the guitar – a source of comfort, of solace – a way to express the angst of teenage years. It was very much a part of me. I still have that guitar today."

As we spoke, Greg's thoughts turned to the enduring lessons of music and how he applies them to the practice of law today.

"Don't be afraid to put yourself in a challenging situation," he advised. "The Beatles [tribute] show was a one-man show, basically undirected. That was a scary thought. The first time I played that, it was like the first time I tried a jury trial. Nobody's holding your hand. You're up there by yourself and you sink or swim. It's all on you."

I found throughout my research that music helped people alleviate the aversion to risk, a catalyst in allowing growth and creativity in any endeavor or personal development process. Greg echoed those sentiments.

"There are a lot of reasons not to breathe deep and jump off the cliff," he said. "There may not be a net, there may not be water, and it may be dangerous. But the most fun you'll ever have is by doing it. If you do it enough, you tend to forget about the ones that we screw up, and you tend to build on the ones that work."

Music has been a catalyst in the development of self-esteem and confidence for most of the people who shared their thoughts on music. Greg articulated how that translates into success in the corporate world.

"In the band I was in, the bass player and I were always in competition over which songs we would do, because that would decide who was singing the song," he said. "If I had just sat back, I would not have had the fun that I had. I would not have been the front man, and I would have been doing songs that somebody else picked that I wasn't that crazy about.

"When you're in a group of people, trust your talent and speak up," he said. "Let your voice be heard. A lot of times there are other people who are making loud noises, and I tend to be kind of shy by nature. When there are those real big, bombastic people who are taking over a social or legal situation, and believe me, there are a lot of bombastic people in the legal profession who like to hear themselves talk, it's easy just to sit back and let them orate."

Very often, it's easy to follow. Taking the lead, especially in a competitive situation, is difficult. Through music, Greg found a way to let his voice be heard, which he believes helped him attain success in all areas of his life.

For Greg, there's an added bonus to being a musical attorney. Some of his clients come to him for legal services specifically because they know that he uniquely understands the plight of the musician.

"I represent a guy who's a guitar player in a band who's got a couple of CDs out, and he's got a lost wage claim because he was in a car accident," Greg said. "He's injured and can't make the same gigs. He felt uncomfortable going to someone who's not a musician because he didn't think they would appreciate how he actually lost money because of this."

The ability to think creatively is the most obvious benefit of music, and Greg shared his thoughts on the creative process. "I find that I am the most creative when I take the time to be alone. You've got to take the time to be by yourself, in total silence, and just think about it, and let stuff come to you. If you're creative, the juices are inside and they flow. You just have to be able to listen to them.

"The creative process, unless you have a collaborator, unless you have a Paul McCartney or a John Lennon to collaborate with, it's a lonely endeavor, and it requires introspection." He added one hint for capturing those ideas when those creative juices begin to flow. "Keep a hand held recorder with you."

Mark Truman, Executive Director & Guitarist/Vocalist

**Executive Director & Founder,
Omniac Education, College entrance
preparedness consulting company
Former Guitarist of the Band Euriska**

"When it comes to success in business, the first place that people fall down and fail is by refusing to own up to their actual dream. Rock bands teach us that the actual dream is to be world famous. To play huge arenas and change people's lives."

* * *

"When people come to business, I wish more of them would say that. Your goal is to change the face of the world through what you do. If more people came to the table like 16 year-old rock musicians, they would find a lot more success and a lot more happiness in the success they find."

Mark Truman is the founder of Omniac Education. His company works almost exclusively with high school students in all aspects of preparation for meeting college entrance requirements. They coach students on standardized testing, assist them in their courses to raise their GPA, help them find appropriate universities, and work through the application process.

Truman had a literature degree and had planned on teaching, but soon realized through his work in the private sector that the public school environment was not for him. He had experience working in the field of private test preparation with both small and large firms. When the owner of a small firm where he was employed passed away, he found himself at a young age in the position of starting up his own company with staff who wanted to continue working in the industry. He carried the lessons of his music experience into the business world, as those events were still very fresh in his mind.

Mark began playing guitar at the age of 16, gravitating toward various forms of folk and acoustic music. In college he formed the band Euriska, and the group progressed for two-and-one-half years from playing outside the dorm to eventually releasing a CD and gaining radio airplay.

According to Mark, the group disbanded prematurely due to what he called "VH-1 *Behind the Music* a little too early," apparently doomed by the pitfalls that usually derail bands much further along the success trail. He continued to play in various projects and continues to sing and play guitar as a sideline to his business pursuits.

Mark claims that early on he didn't listen to music of his generation, and was more influenced by his parents' preference for the "oldies" – The Beatles, the Rolling Stones, and other bands from the 60s.

"My earliest memory was that my dad had purchased all 13 Beatles albums on CD," he recalled. "He was very excited about that and then they got stuck in the CD player. For a year all I could listen to were five Beatles albums – *Revolver, Rubber Soul, Magical Mystery Tour*, and the two discs of *The White Album*," he said as he laughed.

"I remember thinking that they were the best thing in the entire world, and that I had found something really special," he shared, "that I was probably the only person who knew about this stuff – years later finding out that they were widely regarded as the best band ever – that they had changed everything."

The world of music performance opened up for Mark when he was 16 and his stepfather gave him a guitar for Christmas. "I was dumbfounded," he said. "I had never thought about playing guitar before. He was a guitarist, and he thought I would like it. I liked music."

He recalled that his family was planning a trip to Mexico, and he aspired to learn a few songs that he could play around the campfire. Songs such as the Beatles' "Rocky Raccoon" and a few Bob Dylan songs that simply required the ability to play a few chords fit the bill.

"Right away I fell in love with this idea of putting things together and singing and playing at the same time – being able to construct an entire experience for someone," he said. "That's what I came to love later – this idea that for four minutes of your life, we can sort of captivate you and tell a story or interest you in some way. I can entertain you for four minutes and draw you into my emotional world with a song."

Mark was mostly self-taught, though his stepfather helped him learn the basics, and many of the musicians he met in college helped him improve tremendously. He didn't really consider singing in a band until he started playing guitar.

"One of the things you learn very quickly in a band is that there's a shortage of people who are willing to be at the front – do the singing and be the subject of the most criticism," he said. "When we actually did get our album out and people started reviewing it, the harshest thing they had to say was about [the vocals]. Very rarely does somebody point to a guitar part as being particularly bland or not good. It takes a kind of special thick skin to actually get up in front of the audience and sing."

That experience of fronting the band helped him develop a sense of identity and confidence. "I was a huge nerd through middle school and high school," he confided. "I was not the most popular kid. In fact, a couple of my friends joked that when they were in middle school, they would say 'Don't be like Mark Truman' or 'You're being so Mark Truman right now.'

"So when we started playing coffee shops and 30 people would show up, it made me feel like 'I can do something really cool,'" he said of his transformational music experience. "It was a huge self-esteem boost that I could perform, and people would want to hear it. It made me a lot more three-dimensional. That I could write, and I could add something to the world. It definitely formed for me a sense of creative accomplishment – that I could go out there and do whatever I want if I put my mind to it, and have the skills and practice and work hard enough to make it a success."

Mark developed a strong sense of accomplishment from his music experience. "I knew in college I would start a band, and I knew that once we had a band, we would record an album," he said confidently. "That feeling of always being able to accomplish the next goal I got from music, because it was so tangible. You write a song and it's done. That was very empowering for a 16-year-old kid."

Through his music experience, Mark has developed strong sentiments regarding the importance of giving students such creative outlets. "The number one thing that music brings to schools is involving students who would not typically be involved," he concluded. "What I saw from my personal experiences of playing guitar, the guitar class, and working with the musicals and the choir people is that we would have people who were not typically great students investing themselves in a program that got them results. They would show up to class. They would work. They would be ready to perform. And because of that they would be advancing themselves.

"If you boil school down to math, English, and science, you're teaching a lot of material that's very valuable. But you're missing out on some part of the human experience that is equally valuable, which is the creative, artistic side of humanity. It's important that we involve those people too. They're going to need other avenues of expression. What we don't see when we cut music programs or arts programs in general is the cost to students who are not traditionally successful," he concluded.

Reflecting upon his band experience, Mark articulated multiple lessons that carried over into his business experience. "There are so many things – from the branding of a band to the marketing of my business," he said. "From attracting qualified musicians to attracting qualified employees. There's so much that I've learned. The number one thing is that hard work does not automatically equal success on day one.

"When we started our band, we were sure that in six months we'd be world famous," he confided. "We had great music by our standards, we were exciting people, and we were very smart. So what could possibly stop us from being the next great rock band?

"Over the next two years as we slogged it out in tiny clubs nobody cared about and lost members and replaced members and bought better equipment and learned to record and learned to songwrite, what we learned was that nothing comes quickly," he assessed. "But if you're willing to put your nose to the grindstone, it will come eventually."

When Mark started his business, he knew early on that he'd need to do a lot of the same things he had done with his band – brand it, develop a website, contact people and be willing to talk to them about the product he was selling, and connect with the people in his office. He also knew that success was not going to come overnight.

"And that's actually a hard thing for me," he admitted. "I'm a very impatient person. I want to get down to business today. I want to make things happen today. I'm excited and passionate. It has been so invaluable for me to learn that it takes time for something to catch on."

Mark encourages the young students he counsels to find a sense of passion in their lives as well. "I'm a college consultant, and I advise students on what they should do to look good for colleges," Mark explained. "The number one thing that I tell them is do what you love. Find something that's exciting to you and that interests you, because what you play at can say so much about who you are. There's a phrase I always say which is 'Show me what you love, and I'll show you who you are.'"

Mark brings the same sense of passion that was the driving force of his band to his new business. He believes that those who approach their business as merely a way to make a living could learn something from the mind of the musician.

"You're in a band the second you decide to be in a band," he revealed. "You're 16. You get your first guitar, and your buddy also plays guitar. So you form a band," he explained. "You're just looking for a drummer. The band has been formed.

"What I've learned from that is the number one step to success is to just start," he added. "When it comes to success in business, the first place that people fall down and fail is by refusing to own up to their actual dream. Rock bands teach us that the actual dream is to be world famous – to play huge arenas and change people's lives. And most bands that start contain a nugget of that somewhere. They may not admit it right off the bat – 'I wish we could be the next U2 or the next Radiohead or the next Beatles.' We could change the course of rock music.

"When people come to business, I wish more of them would say that," he expressed. "Your goal is to change the face of the world through what you do. If more people came to the table like 16-year-old rock musicians, they would find a lot more success and a lot more happiness in the success they find."

Since Mark is a business owner and took an active role in the direction of the band, I asked whether there were parallels that have shaped his approach to leadership.

"The number one thing that comes to mind is vision," said Mark with respect to leadership. "I was the source of vision for my band. I knew where we were going. I knew what our brand should stand for and what we were going to be as a rock band. That's because I went to every member of the band and said, 'What do you want out if this? How do you contribute to this? How can we build this?' And I knew that there were multiple times when my vision was the number one thing that kept us together.

"When I started managing other people, the vision I knew was the key to making us a successful team," he explained. "Waking up every day and feeling like you're part of something that's more than just a business that collects fees from clients and provides services – that we genuinely make kids lives better because of what we do. If every one of us keep that in mind and behave along those lines, then we actually do that. The same was true with the band. We wanted to provide an experience that was not being provided – the kind of band that people would be excited about."

Mark explained that a band is largely a social experience, and that those social skills will become increasingly important in the 21st century business world. "Social skills come from being forced to work with others, even when sometimes you don't want to. I know there were days when I wanted to rip my band members' heads off. Like 'I can't believe you're opposing me on this. I'm right and you're wrong.' That 'forced togetherness' helps you to learn to get along with others.

"When it comes to being a team [in business] the ability to say, 'You and I want different things. But together we will create something better than we could create apart.' That's incredibly powerful," he concluded. "As globalization becomes a bigger issue as we're working with people farther and farther away from where we live, that continued interest in getting along, working well, and being a team player is going to become more and more important."

David Finch, CEO/Owner & Vocalist/Harmonica Player
CEO & Owner, ATCOM Business Telecom Solutions
Lead Singer, The Dune Dogs

"There are all kinds of lessons [from music]. Getting along, working together, leadership, motivation. A lot of the reputation of musicians is that they're not motivated, and that's just not true. They're extremely motivated."

* * *

"That's what we're looking for in the workforce, motivated people."

David Finch is the CEO and owner of ATCOM Business Telecom Solutions, a full-service business telecommunications firm serving over 5,000 clients ranging in size from approximately 20-250 employees. He worked his way up the company ladder, joining the startup organization right out of school. David was named Vice-President of Sales and Marketing within a few years. In 1996 he was named CEO, and he and his partner bought out the founders of the company.

The privately-held firm is headquartered in Research Triangle Park, with regional offices in Charlotte and Greensboro. ATCOM has twice been named one of North Carolina's Top 50 Technology Companies.

David is also the lead singer and harmonica player for the Dune Dogs, voted the Triangle's best local band of 2007 by *Metro* magazine. The band's sound is characterized as a blend of "hard core country, swamp boogie, and southern rock and roll."

For evidence that musical ability and business acumen can exist in harmony, look no further than the Dune Dogs. David indicates that the band is comprised of two CEOs, another member who founded a company with his dad, an information technology expert, and a commercial real estate broker.

David's mother was a singer, and he followed her example from an early age by singing in the choir and in school plays. He quickly realized a certain sense of accord between performer and audience that made music appealing.

"When you're singing or performing music, there's a spiritual feeling that transcends daily life," he said. "And I say that not from a religious standpoint. It's not necessarily an escape, but it's just a good warm feeling that you're one with the people you're performing with and for, but also the universe as it were. Just a very comforting feeling."

During the last decade, David has discovered the allure of a genre of music known as Americana/Alternative Country. The music has a strong presence in Austin and in Nashville, but also has a following in the Raleigh area. He began to observe artists in small venues, and eventually got involved by sponsoring those performers as they would add Raleigh to their tour schedule. The Nash County Arts Center purchased a small building that was formerly a church. It seats about 180 people, and the wooden interior provides outstanding acoustics and a performance intimacy that is captivating.

"There was another guy in town that loved the same type of music and wanted to bring it out of the bars," David explained. "He went to several companies and solicited sponsorships to cover the costs of the band, and that allowed them to donate any additional proceeds to a local charity. He built a series of acts that he would bring in from Austin and Nashville. He would find out when these acts were coming through the east coast, and he would book them down there.

"Being in an intimate setting and being able to just feel that music – you're just sitting and listening," said David. "It's not a big smoky bar, hell-raising and that kind of thing. That's when I got in touch that it's really poetry set to music versus just a song."

Clearly those shows had an effect on David, rekindling his interest in playing music and igniting a desire to use it as a form of personal expression.

"Several of those shows – I'm getting chill bumps just thinking about Rodney Crowell, Will Kimbrough, Billy Joe Shaver – we've had him there several times," he recalled emotionally. "The really nice thing is that they had an opportunity to explain their songs. That allows the song to take on a whole new meaning. That's when I started writing music – after I attended several of those concerts. I've always written poetry, but I didn't realize that I could take that poetry and make it into music."

I asked David to tap into that reflective side of his personality to articulate the interplay between music and his business success.

"There are two things that you're trying to teach children, and one of them is discipline," he said. "And if you don't think it takes a lot of discipline to learn music – your scales, then you're mistaken. The second thing they don't teach in the schools that we need in the business world is creativity. Music is one of the most creative outlets that human beings have. You don't know what you can do until you try things. Music allows you in the comfort of the practice room to try things you wouldn't ordinarily try."

David also articulated the concept of presence and self-confidence that comes from standing in front of an audience. "It's terrifying. It's not anymore, but it used to be. They say public speaking is the thing that most people are afraid of. That's because most people don't even consider getting up in front of thousands of people and singing."

The Dune Dogs were founded from informal weekend gatherings among friends with some musical training. In both business and in music, David has had the pleasure of watching an idea grow and flourish under his direction.

"Watching a seed of a dream grow into something. You've got four guys who got together and played music on the back deck and made up songs and had a fun weekend. People started coming over and listening to us, and somebody says, 'Why don't you guys play out somewhere?'"

While there's nothing wrong with playing music for enjoyment in your own surroundings, David realized that taking the band to another level required more than musical ability and creativity. It requires vision and a sense of purpose.

"I'm more of a 'Let's look ahead and determine what is our goal. Where are we going with this?'" he noted. "I've seen the potential that we've had. I've emerged as the leader of this band by default. You need people with creativity and passion and motivated to be innovative. If no one comes to hear you, it doesn't matter. That's the defining piece, if you want to play and you want to be successful.

"There are all kinds of lessons [from music]. Getting along, working together, leadership, motivation. A lot of the reputation of musicians is that they're not motivated, and that's just not true. They're extremely motivated. That's what we're looking for in the workforce, motivated people."

Michael Salsburg, Ph.D., Technology Director & Violinist

Chief Architect, Chief Technology Office, UNISYS Corporation
Violinist, Hank's Cadillac & participant in Philadelphia's famous Mummers Parade

"Especially when you play violin – when you first start playing, it doesn't sound so good. The serious people just keep persevering. Obviously, that helps your professional career."

* * *

"The kinds of projects I work on these days can go on for years and years. The Ph.D. in math took me seven years. There were guys who were math geniuses that were way above me, and they never got the degree. I just kept moving along. I picked the pieces and slowly got it done."

Michael Salsburg is the Chief Architect of the Chief Technology Office of Unisys Corporation. Early in his career he worked as a computer programmer with Burroughs Corporation, which later merged with Sperry Univac to become Unisys.

In 1990 he invented software that was used to evaluate computer performance. He later started his own company, Performance & Modeling, Inc., and that company was later purchased by a Silicon Valley company. He stayed on with the parent company as Vice-President of Software through various iterations, but later returned to Unisys when "things cooled off in Silicon Valley," as he described it.

He holds a Masters Degree in Computer Science and a Ph.D. in Mathematics. He has two international patents and lectures worldwide on the topic of computer performance evaluation.

Michael's background is interesting in the sense that he has creative responsibility in a field that is populated with "left-brain" or logical, analytical thinkers. Yet Michael's background in music and his track record of innovation within his field demonstrate the value of music and the arts beyond artistic careers. If we view music and arts education simply as a breeding ground for future artists, we miss the point. The real value lies in the ability of the arts to instill a broader and more creative perspective in all people and in all professions.

Some of Michael's earliest recollections are of his mother sitting at the piano. Not surprisingly, he began to play piano at the age of four. "I heard a lot of interesting music on TV," he recalled with a nostalgic tone. "It was the music on TV that prompted me to sit down and play the piano. I was watching the Mickey Mouse Club, and at the end when they finish with that cool harmony 'M-O-U-S-E' – I'd never heard anything quite like it. I sat down and just started figuring out what the [piano] keys were to make that sound. And that's how it started."

Five years later he migrated to violin so that he could secure a place in the grammar school orchestra, and he continued to play through high school. When he graduated from college he played in a working band. He later moved to Hollywood where he worked for roughly five years (1972-1977) as a professional session musician. He referred to 20s and 30s jazz as his specialty, but acknowledged that as a working musician you learn to play bluegrass, country & western, mariachi, or just about anything.

He currently performs with Hank's Cadillac, a country & western band. He also plays with a Philadelphia string band in the Mummers Parade, a local Philadelphia cultural and social phenomenon.

It wasn't until he was in his twenties and playing professionally that he found an exceptional teacher who helped him clean up his technique and get to the next level. That teacher, Theodore "Ted" Rosen, was a concert master for the David Rose orchestra, known for their work on television's *Red Skelton Show*.

Michael articulated some of the qualities that made Rosen such a memorable teacher. "He was the first who really shared insight into how to practice and how to approach a complex problem," he explained. "That's really a lot of it – understanding how to take a hard piece [of music] and break it down into smaller pieces.

"He was more like a trainer," he added. "He evaluated what I was doing wrong very carefully, and then prescribed exercises to improve. It wasn't just 'you show up every week and you get a bunch of etudes to study and then you play and I'll see you next week.' He took a very personal interest in why I wasn't able to do certain things and then came up with solutions for me. That's very special."

Michael expressed the ways in which music facilitated his development as a youngster. "It was a small community [of friends] – people who went to orchestra went to practice. So I had a feeling of belonging. Otherwise in high school, you could be just floating.

"From a very early age, I realized that it was something that I did better than most people," he added regarding music. "And that meant something, because I wasn't an athlete. I wasn't necessarily the brightest kid. But when it came to music, I could whip them. And I was good. And that really gave me a lot of confidence."

When you research the topic of creativity, one theme that comes up time and time again is that most people have the capacity to be creative. Creativity requires work, however, and you must consistently exercise what I call the "creativity muscle" to ensure that those abilities are developed. You must also believe that you have the capacity to be creative, or else those negative thoughts become a self-fulfilling prophecy. Michael echoed those sentiments regarding the long term commitment that is required to foster creativity.

"I was able to realize a lot of potential regarding creativity, which today is a very important part of my professional life," Michael said. "It's [creativity] something that you have to nurture for a long time. If you cut out the arts and just stick with sports for example, you're cutting out this whole level of creativity that really could end up being very beneficial for the community. By not funding music education, you're not funding the development of creativity in children."

Michael provided his own tips for how to get into a creative mindset, at least the process that works for him. "You've got to learn to quiet your mind," he explained. "You've got to shut out the whole circus around you. And if I can get to a point that I'm thinking of nothing, that's when my best solos happen. I think some of my best innovative technical ideas have happened in those situations when I wasn't thinking about anything and it just bubbled up."

His thoughts also confirmed the idea that you have to believe in your own capacity for creative thought. "There are lots of people who aren't [creative] and don't care," he said. "They like coming to work, doing their job, and going home. Innovation is what I do. I have two international patents. The idea of thinking outside the box – I *am* outside the box. That's how I feel. It's what I am."

He discussed the lesson in perseverance that he learned through music and applied to business. "Especially when you play violin, when you first start playing it doesn't sound so good," he said. "The serious people just keep persevering. Obviously, that helps your professional career. The kinds of projects I work on these days can go on for years and years. The Ph.D. in math took me seven years. There were guys who were math geniuses that were way above me, and they never got the degree. I just kept moving along. I picked the pieces and slowly got it done."

Michael referred to a common theme in my research: the concept of discipline as an outcome of music education.

"When I moved to Hollywood and I was playing professionally, I was practicing about six hours a day," he said. "That takes real discipline. Obviously that's going to spill into your professional career. I now work from a home office, and I worked at home for 12 years prior to coming back to Unisys. I've had no problem disciplining myself to do the work rather than doing laundry and other things. There are a lot of people who can't do that.

"That's [in music] where I learned it – all the discipline it takes to practice and to participate in orchestras."

On the topic of passion and conviction, Michael closed with a story that exemplifies the ability of the musician to demonstrate those qualities and to extrapolate them to other endeavors. "We set up a whole strategic program around this vision I had outlined at Unisys," he explained. "When I get a team on the phone, all I'm doing is telling them in a very passionate way how I feel about something. But it comes through. It's really passion. It's not just 'Get the job done.'"

Dianne Sclafani, Small Business Consultant & Vocalist
Sclafani Cooking School
Small Business & Restaurant Consultant
Vocalist

"It [music] gave me a lot of confidence, a lot of presence. I've been in sales many years, and I feel like it prepared me to take on challenges and to be in competition. Really a well-roundedness and a feel for how to understand what people want."

* * *

"Music requires discipline. It teaches you focus. I think it's so important for kids to be exposed to that, because I think it does help you in later years in whatever field you go into. You can put that into sales, engineering, and even medicine."

Dianne Sclafani comes from a family of restaurateurs in the New Orleans area. Her grandfather started Sclafani's Restaurant in New Orleans in 1945. Her father followed that tradition, and the family moved the restaurant out to a sprawling suburban area of the city in 1958, where it remained until 1985.

Since that time, Dianne and her family have operated Sclafani Cooking School, Inc., an intensive four-week baker and cook certification program that prepares workers for careers in the restaurant business. Dianne somehow finds time to serve as a small business consultant for restaurant owners and as a professional speaker, having served as President of the National Speakers Association New Orleans chapter in 2004-05.

The family restaurant served as host to a "Who's Who" of celebrities and musicians passing through New Orleans for a span of 40 years. It also served as a playground for Dianne, an aspiring young performer growing up in the Big Easy with a new audience every night.

"Going back to our restaurant days before my time in the 40s, all of the opera singers that were performing at the opera house would come to our restaurant, and they would get up and sing there," Dianne said. "Definitely music was running through the family and the business. By the time I came around in the early 60s, we still had a lot of movie stars coming into town that would come to our restaurant, and I got to meet them. A lot of them were musicians.

"And because Metairie (a suburb of the greater New Orleans metro area) was just starting to form, all of the fashion shows for the department stores were coming around," she explained. "There was a stage built at our restaurant to feature their fashion shows. That's when I really got the stage bug. I would entertain our employees and customers and anybody I could get to look my way. And I'd sing and dance and do whatever I could. So that was my true playground as a kid."

Dianne recalled some of the recognizable names of the restaurant patrons, some of whom she met personally and some of whom passed through before her time.

"I remember one that impressed me because I was 12 years old at the time was Frankie Avalon," she recalled. "At that time they would show those beach movies in the middle of the day, so he was still pretty big. Frank Sinatra had come to our restaurant. A lot of people who were famous in New York would come down here from the Metropolitan. Mario Lanza frequented our restaurant before my time. Eleanor Steber was very good friends with my grandparents. She was a famous opera singer who performed at the Met and taught at Juilliard. People like Rock Hudson and Roy Rogers."

Dianne recalled that her family always seemed to have an affinity for music and supported the arts. "Most all of my uncles played some instrument in the school band," Dianne said. "My grandfather played the violin, and my great-grandmother was a great advocate of the opera and loved classical music. When my grandfather was a baby, she would sneak him into the opera under her cape, because she didn't have a babysitter."

Dianne recalled cherished memories that connected her with her father in a memorable way. "I remember being four years old and just loving the stage and loving everything musical," she said with delight. "I just felt that I had a connection. Being in the restaurant business, to see my father I would stay up late at night. The television stations would sign off with the Star Spangled Banner, and I have fond memories singing with him as the stations were signing off."

Dianne explored various instruments including clarinet, guitar, and trumpet, yet she always gravitated toward vocal. "In the band they always persuaded you to be whatever they needed, but I just felt a calling to the vocal part," she said.

So Dianne pursued vocal studies, receiving encouragement from music teachers to take voice seriously. "In high school my teacher had recommended that I go to state competition," said Dianne. "That's when I started taking private lessons through Loyola University with one of the teachers there who was very well-regarded, Mary Tortorich."

With Ms. Tortorich's encouragement, Dianne pursued music and received a scholarship to the University of New Orleans. She studied there for about a year, but the demands of trying to juggle her responsibilities in the restaurant business and music studies proved limiting. She later went back as a part-time music student and performed in musical theater there as well.

Still, Dianne has taken powerful lessons from her musical background that laid the foundation for her success, including a defining moment from that state competition that she shared with me.

"I was maybe 15 or 16 years old," Dianne recollected. "I just didn't have the confidence that I thought I probably needed at that time in music. But she [her high school teacher] encouraged me that it was my time to go into competition. It was at Louisiana State University. They had the rooms all set with the judges. It was my first real experience in formal judging. These people were so plain-faced, and I didn't know that they were told to be that way – not to show any emotion or bias. I grew up in a very different environment.

"This one fellow who was a little older than most had learned the system," Dianne recalled vividly. "If he could make the rest of the people in the competition nervous, they would not do as well, and his performance would surely ring out the loudest. He came out of the room after he had been through his competition, and he just said how awful everybody was and how tough it was. You could see everyone in the hall was just about shaking; they were so nervous and taken aback from all that this fellow was saying.

"So I went in there, and I see these judges with a look of, 'Yeah, just try to impress us.' I actually sang out of the window. There was a beautiful oak tree and I said, 'Well, if I'm going to get through this, I need an audience.' So I sang to the tree. My comments were that I had a lot of potential, and with training I would do much better. They gave me okay scores," Dianne admitted.

"I needed that year to grow up and mature," she presumed. "When I came back the next year, I had figured out what my little fellow was about. He pulled his same stunt, trying to scare everybody. I said, 'He's not going to scare me this time. Been there, done that.' So I went in there, and I gave it my best shot. I won the solo as well as two ensembles medals," Dianne said proudly.

"So I felt that that was quite an accomplishment. It really taught me not to let people persuade you. You have to find out things on your own."

Dianne articulated many of the benefits of music that have translated into career success outside of music, of which there are many in her estimation. "It gave me a lot of confidence, a lot of presence," she stated. "I've been in sales many years, and I feel like it prepared me to take on challenges and to be in competition. Really a well-roundedness and a feel for how to understand what people want.

"I think it's helped me in school, in business," she added. "It's helped me to organize things. Music requires discipline. It teaches you focus. I think it's so important for kids to be exposed to that, because I think it does help you in later years in whatever field you go into. You can put that into sales, engineering, and even medicine. It's all the same skill sets that we need to do a great job. And I think music can really develop that in people."

It is said that in New Orleans people carry around musical instruments like people in Manhattan carry brief cases. Therefore, music can provide a vehicle for initiating relationships conducive to business success. "Especially being from New Orleans," said Dianne, "You can usually find some connection with people through music. Either they play or sing. Sometimes when you can't necessarily sell it any other way, you can do it through music."

I also asked Dianne to articulate the importance of music on a more personal level, irrespective of the benefits in a business context.

"It was a connection with people," Dianne shared. "At that time I was an only child. The [restaurant] customers and employees were my playmates. It was a way for me to connect and get attention in a talented way. It was something that I could share personally. It wasn't something that my family was giving to the customers. It was a part of who I was. And I still feel that way. When I sing, it's me. It's like a little gift. Right now the majority of what I sing is in church. It's a gift back to my fellowship in the church. It's very spiritual."

As a speaker, Dianne utilizes music as a tool for facilitating the learning process during speeches, workshops, and training events. She explained the effectiveness of using music in such a manner.

"People will remember it was an emotional message, but they won't always remember the message if it is done verbally all of the time," Dianne explained. "When it's done with music, they remember it on a different level. They remember the emotion behind it. They remember the message. I saw somebody recently who saw me speak several years ago. He said, 'I remembered when you sang.' He remembered what I was trying to convey.

"I think through music, they get it," she added. "It's almost like a little jingle. They go around singing it during class. They just absorb it immediately. I don't know if it's just because it's a different way of learning, but they don't have to be musicians to understand it. It is very effective. It relaxes people so that they can learn."

When asked if she had any additional thoughts for the readers, Dianne left me with a few parting thoughts on the subject of the joy of music. "Just that people always remember to have music in their heart. I find that sometimes we tend to get very serious in our work. And music brings out that kid and that play that we all have that lets us enjoy life," she warmly stated.

"It's a universal language."

The Idea Factories

*Business Leaders with
Music Backgrounds Working
in Creativity Fields*

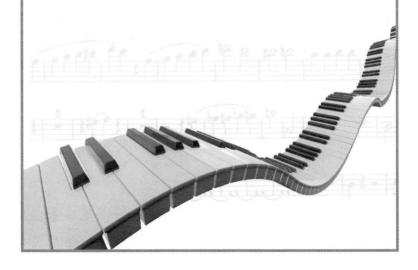

Andrew Mackenzie, CEO & Guitarist
CEO, Yamamoto, Moss, Mackenzie,
branding agency
Guitarist

"You stand at a whiteboard in front of a bunch of clients that are ready to tear you to shreds. You have to be confident to move forward with an idea. You have to be confident to lead in a business way in some direction that you think is going to be right. You're in the middle of the song, you've got your guitar in your hands, and you know you're in [the key of] 'B.' Ready, go!"

* * *

"That moment of 'What am I going to do here? What am I going to play here?' is absolutely the same as standing at a whiteboard. You've got an audience. The audience wants to know what you're going to do...They can both be hostile. You really have to trust your team. You have to trust your creativity, and you have to be willing to take a risk."

Andrew Mackenzie is the CEO of Yamamoto, Moss, Mackenzie, a full service branding agency out of Minneapolis, MN. He has spent 20 years building marketing strategies, promotions, and product introductions. He started Mackenzie in 1997, grew it quickly, and eventually sold the firm. The companies for whom Andrew worked prior to starting his own firm include McCaffrey & McCall and Chase Manhattan bank.

Over a 20 year span, Andrew has helped senior executives design and build marketing strategies, promotions, and product introductions that have generated billions in sales. The firm's clients include Cargill, Macy's, Royal Caribbean, General Mills, Pillsbury, P&G, Target, and St. Jude Medical.

Andrew indicated that he began playing guitar from the time that he was 'in double digits' and in bands since he was 18. "The funny thing about bands when you get older is that garage bands really turn into nice wet bar basement bands," he said with amusement. "Everybody's gotten older and has a little bit better means. What was the garage becomes the really nice, furnished, wall-to-wall carpeted wet bar that everybody gets to hang out in and play every Wednesday night.

"We also have a company band which is terrific," he added. "Right now we're trying to find another guitar player, because we had all of the pieces, and we have a wonderful basement here in this building where we've set everything up. It's nice to get multiple bands going. It's just like working in multiple teams. Every one brings out something different in you."

Andrew drifted back to his early days and recalled a day in Stowe, Vermont when the seeds of his rock and roll dreams were planted. "This kid who I was hanging out with whom I didn't know – we're sitting there staring at each other at some ski lodge, wondering what the heck to do, and if we really wanted to talk to each other," he reminisced. "He put on a KISS album. It was the first KISS album, and I heard 'Cold Gin,' 'Firehouse,' and 'Strutter.' It just got you at sort of a guttural level. I've been a rock hound ever since."

From there, Andrew's cousins and brothers would give him various albums by bands such as Led Zeppelin and Little Feat. He then discovered Discomat in New York where he could get albums for $5.99, which enabled him to build a substantial album collection.

Once bitten, Andrew discovered a connection that allowed him to explore the gamut of rock music of the day. "My mother was the Leader Writer (a senior journalist) for *Newsweek* magazine," he explained. "Once I got the bug, I went in, and I talked to the head writer for the music section there. They used to get so many demo albums. She let me go through hundreds of albums that the record companies had given her and take anything I wanted."

From that point onward, Andrew was focused on rock music, and efforts by others to direct him toward a more mellow sound were futile.

"I'd go to school and learn 'Blowin' in the Wind,' and then I'd get home," he said of his routine. "I'd go down to the store. This was before tabs (guitar tablature), before anything really cool, and I'd buy music books. Then I'd sit there trying to figure out how to play 'Smoke on the Water,' wailing away on the single string – anything just to get something past the folk songs that she [his fifth grade teacher] was teaching us."

While playing the distortion-based rock songs of his era on acoustic guitar presented its challenges, it was in college that Andrew was quite literally "electrified" by guitar. "I had a room-mate, Mark Jones, who had been in bands and was absolutely a cool rocker. He stuck an electric guitar in my hands, plugged me in, and it was love from then on with the instrument."

Sometimes just a minimal bit of guidance from an instructor can open up an entire world of musical possibilities to the student. Andrew had one such experience.

"I took lessons at The New School (University) in New York from a guy named Steve Tarshin," he recalled. "It sounds like such a minor thing, but he taught me the minor pentatonic scale. Learning the minor pentatonic scale, as you know, is pretty much most everything in rock guitar. You can play almost any-thing. He taught me that and he taught me how to slide between the connections. That little piece of vocabulary, that tiny bit of music unlocked so many songs that I could play, have fun with, and just riff over."

Sometimes the key to effective music education lies in revealing to the student a balance of the required fundamentals of practice and a joyous vision of the fruits of hard work.

"I've got a boy that plays piano, and he was absolutely dying, being drilled on how to read, read, read, read, read," said Andrew. "I said just pick your favorite piece, and he picked Vince Guaraldi (the jazz pianist widely known as the composer of the music that accompanied the Peanuts cartoons). We did that, and we did the theme from Star Wars. Suddenly, he was digging what he was playing. He was willing to go back and read, because he was then inspired. If you don't mix in inspiration, I think all that it becomes is boot camp."

Andrew was very clear regarding the value of exposure to music in preparing him for his professional career.

"There are three principles in music that absolutely, positively overlap in business," he concluded. "One is that concept of teamwork. The second is creativity within that team and trust that's developed. And the third is spontaneity."

For Andrew, the obvious benefit of music education that correlates to the corporate sector is the capacity for original thought.

"It's all about creativity – being able to express yourself," he said. "I can't draw worth beans, but give me a guitar and I can hopefully take you to someplace with me that you're going to have a good time. I'm a geeky CEO of a brand agency, and I can do numbers until the cows come home. But my creative outlet throughout my life has been to take a piece of (guitar) string, have it vibrate, and take you emotionally to a place that I couldn't with any other form of art. It's always been my way of expressing myself, outside of ones and zeros in the computer and things that line up in numbers.

"You stand at a whiteboard in front of a bunch of clients that are ready to tear you to shreds," he said of the perils of his vocation.

"You have to be confident to move forward with an idea. You have to be confident to lead in a business way in some direction that you think is going to be right. You're in the middle of the song, you've got your guitar in your hands, and you know you're in [the key of] 'B.' Ready, go!

"That moment of 'What am I going to do here? What am I going to play here?' is absolutely the same as standing at a whiteboard," he added regarding the overt parallels. "You've got an audience. The audience wants to know what you're going to do. One's a little more hostile than the other, but not always. They can both be hostile. You really have to trust your team. You have to trust your creativity, and you have to be willing to take a risk."

Andrew believes that if people don't have some sort of creative outlet, they are less inclined to take risks. "You can always tell the people that are willing to lay themselves out creatively. Those are the people that you want on your team, because they're willing to share ideas," he said. "They are going to be willing to go to someplace you haven't been to before that's new, and not just what they've heard. The world is full of creators and editors. Editing is the easy way in life, because you go through giving your opinion on somebody else's work. Creating is hard because you've got to fill a blank page. In music, you've got to fill an empty stage, and you're out for ridicule."

Andrew explained that trusting your creative partners to demonstrate the fearlessness required to generate new ideas is critical in his business, and again he provided a parallel from his music experience.

"You know when you get to an open session where you're not just going 1-2-3 through a song, but you're just sort of riffing and everybody's playing off of each other," he illuminated. "Those spontaneous moments of creativity are about trust that your drummer's going to be there for you doing what they do. Whoever's playing horns is going to come through with some cool riff, and they're not going to mind if you suddenly kick in a wah-wah [guitar effects] pedal. In business, you're working on a team, and if one person has to be the lead all of the time, if one person always has to be the dominant one, if you're not going to trust the person to express themselves, [you won't be successful]. You have the same elements of trust, teamwork, and creativity that you have to apply, whether it's in business or in music."

And Andrew expressed with some degree of frustration the inability of some people to make that correlation and to recognize those benefits of music education that transcend the arts. "You have to see how music is not something that is a convenience, but it is a core expression of how we live our lives and of our ability to expand and be successful. You can't just see it as a 'nice to have,' it's a 'need to have.' It's a part of who we are in our core.

"'A' – don't think of it as an elective," he added. "Think about it as core learning. 'B' – there are many, many people who learn to emote and express themselves through music, and the last thing you want is a teenager who has all of their emotions bottled up inside of them. Because you never know which way it's going to squeeze out. 'C' – if the purpose of the school is to be growing community and helping people to work with each other, there is no better way to create common bonds than through the expression of music.

"It [music] is about expression and unformed thinking," Andrew articulated. "It is all about right brain. You play slide guitar and you are on a very slippery plane that has nothing to do with numbers. So the right brain aspect of expression is completely connected in business. We're not just about adding numbers up, but we're about the creativity. And more and more and more, as science and math become commodities, because *things* can do it so quickly for you, what are you doing to come up with something new and different that will resonate with your audience, whether it's business or music?

"You have to ask yourself, 'How are we taught to do that?'" he added. "The next logical question is, 'Where do we get the opportunity to practice that?'"

Andrew closed with his recollection of a film excerpt that illustrated the concept of the musician demonstrating spontaneity, individuality, and originality.

"Do you remember the movie *Rock Star*?" he asked. "Mark Wahlberg (the actor portraying the lead character, Chris 'Izzy' Cole) is in the choir with his girlfriend, and they're singing Hallelujah, Hallelujah. At the end he gives this *huuuuuge* Hallelujah, and they all giggle. To me it's such a perfect example of what happens – everyone talks about 'outside the box thinking,' and it gets so hackneyed, but in that construct of everybody doing harmonies and fifths or whatever they're doing, suddenly he comes out of nowhere with this gigantic emotional flood of how he feels about the song. It's the perfect demonstration of how music helps somebody step outside the box, even in a very tight, methodical, mathematical framework.

"And the people in business who do that are the ones that stand out," he added in closing. "The ones who send the cover letter that sounds like everybody else are the ones who get ignored. The ones who demonstrate creativity and expression are the ones that get noticed."

S. Neil Vineberg, President & Guitarist
**President, Vineberg Communications,
public relations firm
Guitarist (recording and performing credits
include Whitney Houston, Carlos Santana,
& Narada Michael Walden)**

*"Later in life, when companies started to put a
million or two million dollars behind some of my
projects, I would always go back to music – the
idea that if I believed in myself and just played what I felt in music – just
play it and feel it, it's going to be great. I realized that I could apply that
in business, too."*

* * *

*"As I started to look back on my life experiences in business, I realized that
the best work that I had done was created spontaneously and flowed."*

S. Neil Vineberg is the founder and President of Vineberg
Communications, a boutique public relations firm that prides
itself on its hands-on, flexible approach to customer service.
His clients include Sprint, Texas Instruments, Procter & Gamble,
Hershey Foods, CVS.com, CBS Marketwatch, Bausch and Lomb,
United Airlines, IBM, and Sony.

Neil is also an exceptional musician, having recorded with
Whitney Houston and performed with Carlos Santana. He has
also collaborated with Grammy-winning producer and songwriter Narada Michael Walden.

While Neil was a childhood prodigy in music from an early age, an epiphany facilitated by Narada Michael Walden transformed Neil's musical pursuits from vocational to inspirational.

Narada (formerly Michael Walden) invited Neil to a meditation session with a spiritual group under the direction of the guru Sri Chinmoy. The experience was not only inspirational, it was life-changing.

"Sri Chinmoy is a spiritual teacher who's inspired thousands of people to develop their own potential, to find more meaning in their life, and hopefully to live their lives in ways that make the world a better place," Neil explained. "I resonated with him. He made such a profound impact on my life that my first inclination was gratitude. I didn't just want to just sit there being thankful. I wanted to put my gratitude into action by doing something for him.

"Meeting him was transformational in that I essentially learned from him the meaning of life in a way that I could resonate with it and action it in my own existence."

Neil came away from that experience with a strong desire to promote the guru and to spread the word of his message. He spoke to public relations professionals and brainstormed publicity projects that would allow access to radio and television. He began to reach out to political leaders and other influential people. He began "eventizing" Sri Chinmoy's message through running and cycling events that promoted self-transcendence and world peace.

Neil found that he was quite effective at public relations activities and later went to work for UNICEF before founding his own firm.

It was apparent early on that Neil also had a gift for music.

"I was thought to be kind of like a prodigy," he recalled. "As I got older I discovered Beethoven, Bach, Chopin, and Mozart, and I realized that I was a fairly ordinary fellow."

Yet ordinary musical ability is relative, and Neil clearly outpaced his peers. He recalled that he would sit and bang his hands to the beat of music. His mother saw his potential and initiated piano lessons at the age of five. Neil was also gifted with perfect pitch and was essentially playing by ear by the age of seven.

He lacked the focus at that age to listen to his instructor and learn to read music, and he also considered himself somewhat rebellious. At that point he decided to quit piano and take up the guitar. His talent became somewhat of a novelty in school, and he became a showpiece for the music teacher. "At the age of seven I could hear a song on the radio and just play it. And that startled people. I remember being in kindergarten and the music teacher would take me up to the sixth grade class to play guitar."

Ultimately for Neil, music was a social experience. "It was the way I learned discipline," he said. "It was how I made progress as a person, because I had to practice every day. I loved music. It was the most enjoyable and safest environment for me. But I never saw myself as a star. I never saw myself as an artist. I never aspired for name and fame."

But talent did bring with it a certain level of name and fame for Neil. "I was playing in a professional band on TV at the age of ten," he said. "I didn't know anything else. I hadn't thought of what I wanted to do. I was so good at music that I could write my ticket with my eyes closed. There was nothing that I needed to care about, even in school. Where other kids had to worry about grades and career, I could use my own natural [musical] ability."

Even though Neil decided not to make music his vocation, he still draws from his musical training when he approaches public relations and marketing projects. Therefore, he has strong sentiments regarding the funding of music education.

"Learning information the way it's taught in schools, which is essentially memorizing and regurgitating, is a very one-dimensional thing," he explained. "Listening to, performing, discovering, feeling, and expressing music is almost like nature itself unfolding inside of you. To deny people that world of discovery seems to be bordering on criminal.

"I can remember playing in a wind ensemble in high school," he recalled. "I remember performing these pieces, one in particular by Percy Grainger, and playing it and listening to how wonderful it was. I didn't know why it was amazing. I just knew it was amazing. It took me a much longer time to understand the theory and the brilliance and the genius behind creative expression. But just listening to that as a kid was a monumental experience – kind of like when I found my experience of God while meditating. It was a similar thing in music – experiencing music in high school."

Neil believes in the importance of children having the opportunity to do music both as a means of growth and self-discovery, because as he said, "Somewhere among those kids are the next geniuses."

I found Neil's comments regarding the intuitive nature of creative projects in business and the parallels with his musical training to be particularly insightful.

"The great composers had this amazing music coming through them, and they were almost transcribing what they felt and what they heard," he explained. "It was a very natural flow. I find that in the most successful business projects that I create and implement, there's the same kind of organic quality to it that makes great music and also makes great work.

"There is natural order to the universe – a way to find the organic flow to music and flow to life. It's the same way when I am improvising on the guitar. There was a time when I had to construct improvisations. Now I just flow. I don't think about it. I just play.

"I've actually had the same kind of experience in business," he analogized. "A lot of public relations starts with creativity where you have to come up with ideas that might work for a company, and then you have to implement them. So it's the same thing as coming up with the seed of an idea in music and then executing it into a form, either an ensemble or a solo piece.

"I find that if you're trying to create a presence for a company so that the public in general are aware of them, there are musical links that come forward," he added. "There's a rhythm to a company's communications outreach. There's rhythm, there's volume, and there's sometimes big sound. If a company has a brand, that brand is made up of various elements, but not all of them can play at the same volume or at the same intensity. It's the combination of those elements that help to sustain and perpetuate the brand and hopefully impact the market or the customers in unique and hopefully phenomenal ways. And I don't know many people that think about marketing and P.R. in terms of music. I do."

In addition to trusting his instincts, Neil also has developed a confidence in his abilities that is a prerequisite for running your own business and advising Fortune 500 companies. Again he traces the roots of that confidence to his musical training.

"As I started to really work hard and stay focused and come up with new ideas and implement them, generally they were successful," he said. "Later in life when companies started to put a million or two million dollars behind some of my projects, I would always go back to music – the idea that if I believed in myself and just played what I felt in music – just play it and feel it, it's going to be great. I realized that I could apply that in business too.

"As I started to look back on my life experiences in business, I realized that the best work that I had done was created spontaneously and flowed. And that all I have to do is 'do what I do' and it was going to be successful. I just needed to walk forward."

As Neil mentioned previously, music was a social experience, and he capitalizes on that experience in his business endeavors as well.

"I learned so much about teamwork and collaboration and leadership by playing in a band," he said assuredly. "Because I had perfect pitch, even though I was often three years younger than the guys in the band with me, I was always the leader of the band from the age of 10 or 11 on. I learned to teach, because at the age of 16 I was teaching upwards of 20 people weekly to play guitar. I learned pedagogy at the age of 16. I learned how to teach and educate. I learned how to take care of my students and move them along."

It has been my experience from years in the consulting business that people who act as advisors to other organizations must have the ability to convey a sense of calm – a feeling that they are making a wise decision in entrusting certain functions of their operation in an outside entity. They must walk away from meetings with the confidence that the consultant or advisor has things under control.

Conversing with Neil gives you the impression that he possesses that quality, at least in part attributed to his meditation practices.

"The value of meditation is that it helps people develop clarity and calmness," he confided. "I attribute the inspiration for all the work that I do and my success to grace and a higher power.

I approach the blessings of my life with a lot of gratitude and humility.

"I would counsel anybody to essentially find a way to rise above the mind and get into the heart," he added. "Develop calmness and peace of mind. In that space, creativity emerges. Once you are able to navigate that, you can get into the right preparation for the work that you need to do.

"When I need to get ideas, I'm not sitting there racking my brain with pen and paper. I'm just basically sitting calmly and meditating. At this point I have a pretty good access point into the world of ideas."

Neil seems to have found a place for music in his life that complements his transcendental nature. He still plays music, has a recording studio in his home, and continues to collaborate with others. He has migrated his own music into a more spiritual dimension, from pop and commercial into more eastern based music. "I try to stay active. I don't do it for money," he stated. "I'm basically here to inspire, contribute, and share."

Greg Estes, V.P. of Marketing & Keyboard Player

**Vice-President of Marketing, Mozes, Inc.,
mobile marketing technology company
Keyboard Player, Songwriter formerly of the
band Mystery Date**

*"To this day, it [music] is the driving sense of self
that I have. I still think of myself as a musician with
a day job, not a Silicon Valley marketing executive."*

* * *

*"Being successful is not about being the best musician. There's some-
body singing in a bar that's a better piano player than Billy Joel or Elton
John. You learn that and apply that to business as well. You can have the
absolute best technology or the best product or service, but it comes
down to brand awareness and getting noticed in the marketplace."*

Greg Estes is the Vice-President of Marketing at Mozes, a startup company that helps bands, sports teams, clubs, and brand
agencies share text messages, voice messages, and other mobile
content with their fans and customers. He is a veteran of innovative technology and entertainment companies, primarily in
marketing capacities.

Greg has served as Chief Marketing Officer of Silicon Valley
Companies that have been on the cutting edge of video graphics technology. He was a founding member of RasterOps
Corporation, which developed the first 24-bit color and video
technology for the Macintosh computer in the 80s.

"In my music career I'd spent a bunch of time in recording studios writing music for industrial videos or working with video people there trying to do sound effects," Greg explained. "I learned video at two o'clock in the morning with my sleeves rolled up as opposed to theoretically. I kind of knew what the customers wanted and had an affinity for it. They [RasterOps Corporation] made me the video product manager. Once I got into marketing, I was really successful at that."

He was soon lured away for a similar position at Silicon Graphics, Inc., and he saw the potential of the company to expand into new markets, particularly the film and entertainment industries. "They were just selling to scientists and engineers, and I said, 'Oh, my God, you've got something special here for animators and for Hollywood,'" Greg said. "We almost single-handedly created SGI in the entertainment industry through *Jurassic Park* and all of that stuff. I spent a big chunk of my career there."

Greg's most recent position prior to Mozes was that of Chief Marketing Officer of Avid Technology, a company with multiple brands and a leading position in the video editing of film and television. "It's funny, when I went there I felt like I was genetically bred for that job, being a musician, being in marketing, and working in that intersection of media and technology," he said.

When I spoke to Greg he had recently stepped down from Avid. A new CEO had brought in a new regime, and the self-described California kid tired of the travel to Boston. It was a good time for him to reflect on his career and to assess the terms of his success.

Greg achieved a respectable level of success in the music business in the Bay area, enough that on a couple of occasions he flirted with the kind of acclaim that might have redirected his career.

"I started playing in local bands at 14, mostly cover bands up through the time that I was in high school," he recalled. "Then I started to do more studio work. I played on records by a bunch of people you've never heard of. In the early 80s and throughout most of the 80s I had some success in a band called Mystery Date. In the 80s Huey Lewis and the News and The Greg Kihn Band were the kings of the club bands in the Bay area, and we would open for those guys. We had enough success that we would open in the better clubs for national touring acts that would come through.

"We'd get our song played on the radio once in a while, but we never got signed or had that success," he added. "But it was close enough for me that the carrot was kind of always there that kept you doing it. My songwriting partner and I got very close to getting a cut on the second Whitney Houston album. If we would have gotten that cut I wouldn't be talking to you today."

Greg compared the experience to being a triple A baseball player – you never get to the majors, but you have enough success to keep you motivated. During that time his day job got bigger and better, and he started a family. And while the rock star dream didn't quite come to fruition, he has continued to play in cover bands. He has a studio in his house and still collaborates with a songwriting partner.

Greg grew up in what he called a three-parental unit, his two grandparents and his mother. There was a bit of a musical streak in his family. His grandfather could play as many as nine instruments and had a tremendous ear for music. The family owned a piano and an organ, and his grandfather could just start playing any song the adults in the family would name.

"I almost had a writer's block when it came to reading music," said Greg. "What I did have was that same talent [as his grandfather]. I can play almost anything by ear. I play a whole bunch of different instruments."

Greg's son is a drummer, but he has also demonstrated the propensity to pick up new instruments and learn on the fly. "He can play 'Sweet Child of Mine' (by Guns and Roses) on the ukulele," said Greg.

Greg had the desire to play drums and recalled using his mattress as an improvised drum set while playing along with Grand Funk Railroad's "We're an American Band." His mother squashed the idea of bringing a drum set into the house, and Greg seemed to have an aptitude for the keys anyway.

"I think because we had keyboards around the house, once I started playing piano it was clear that I was much more natural on that instrument."

Greg describes himself as a huge Beatles fan, and took four years of formal piano lessons. "My piano teacher to his great credit, instead of beating my head and his head against the wall and trying to get me to read music – he would hear me play things that were kind of tenth year Chopin from a third year student, and he just recognized that my natural ability greatly exceeded my ability to read," Greg explained. "So he kind of gave up on me in some ways and he decided to teach me theory. That really helped to amplify my ear and my natural ability to play. That was a huge influence on me. I'm really grateful he had that kind of insight."

Though music took a bit of a back seat to his full-time job, he has always considered himself a musician first, and his friends would agree. "To this day, it [music] is the driving sense of self that I have. I still think of myself as a musician with a day job, not a Silicon Valley marketing executive."

Greg discussed the parallels of the dynamics of running a band and running an organization. "There are things that you apply to work," he said. "There's this weird kind of democracy that happens in a band where it's all volunteer work. And there's usually no anointed leader, which means that you've got to find a way to make space for everybody and have them contribute and feel good about it, without simultaneously being directionless.

"You learn how to make it so that contributions are valued, while you also don't necessarily think of all of those contributions at the same level of hierarchy," he explained. "Your bass player is clearly not the best player in the band. You've got to figure out 'Are we going to try to make him a better bass player, are we going to change our music around so that his level of bass is the right level of simplicity for the kind of music we're doing, or are we going to bite the bullet and kick him out?'

"Think of that in the business context. You have somebody that's working for you on your team. You've got somebody who's struggling. You've got to figure out, 'Am I going put the energy in to bootstrap this person up so that they're going to perform at the correct level, or is the level of work that they're doing going to work out for us?'"

He spoke of the experience of developing relationships with other musicians, working toward a common goal, and the lessons learned at a young age.

"A lot of your lasting friendships come from people that you play with in bands – that bonding experience that you have of shared interest and being in a band and working through tough times, providing a creative outlet linking that to deep friendships, plus meeting new people and becoming friends with them as your musician circle grows," he said. "And then learning life's lessons, overcoming hurdles and obstacles, having the joy of getting on television or hearing your song on the radio or playing a large amphitheater – whatever happens to you in your career – all of those things tied back to music and started at a very early age."

Greg conveyed a very specific nuance of branding and positioning in the marketplace, and the parallels between musicians and their audience and companies and their customers.

"I think about innovation," he explained. "As a company you need to continually innovate. You've got to do that while not shocking the marketplace. As a marketing guy, you might say, 'We need the marketplace's permission to go and do that.' You can't have a tire company come out with a new line of perfume.

"You learn that same lesson as a musician coming up, particularly when you have more and more success," he said. "People start to expect that you as an artist are supposed to sound 'this way.' At some point maybe you're so big and you've got your own momentum like Madonna, for instance. Then you can reinvent yourself at will because the flywheel is going on your own career. Other people might alienate some of their marketplace.

"Figuring out how to change and adapt to change and be able to embrace it extremely carefully and understand what the marketplace is willing to accept from you – I'm not sure that musicians would necessarily think of it that way, but with the perspective of a business guy, I look at that and say, 'Wow, that's almost the same thing.'"

With the viewpoint of a marketing executive, Greg understands the importance of getting noticed in the marketplace, and again he traced those roots to his music experience.

"Being successful is not about being the best musician," he said. "I don't know that Jewel is the best singer in the United States or the best songwriter in the United States. There's somebody singing in a bar that's a better piano player than Billy Joel or Elton John. What it's about is being noticed. People say it's about being at the right place at the right time. You kind of make your own serendipity in a lot of ways.

"You learn that and apply that to business as well," he explained. "You can have the absolute best technology or the best product or service, but it comes down to brand awareness and getting noticed in the marketplace. It could be through P.R. It could be through advertising. It could be through a variety of different ways.

"That is one thing that I definitely learned from my music ca-reer. Just being great doesn't necessarily mean that you're going to be successful," he concluded. "You can't just go back and practice for another 13 hours a day and suddenly get signed. In the same way it may not be about making a product with 12 new features or cutting your price by 32%. You've got to find ways to get into the public eye, get noticed, and make sure people are out there."

Greg also alluded to the importance of dedication and diligence combined with patience, given the fact that the time lapse be-tween your efforts and the associated rewards can sometimes be significant. "It takes an enormous amount of practice and hard work before you get that one moment in time where you go on stage," he said. "You do that before you're getting that immediate reward, not getting the immediate gratification of the ultimate prize. You have to put an awful lot of work into it before you're far enough down the road that you get to show the benefit of that work and therefore get the recognition or payback, or whatever it is.

"That's true in product development of almost any kind of prod-uct or service," he explained. "That's a great overall lesson for business as well."

Because Greg's success has come in the field of technology re-sulting from his interest in and understanding of the evolution of the capabilities of keyboards and synthesizers, it's hard to extri-cate his career from his music.

"I would go out on a limb and say that I would attribute almost all of my success [to music] – from work ethic, to figuring ways to be creative and come up with new ideas, to how I deal with people as a people manager, to the types of jobs I've been able to get because I'm a keyboard player. I've had to be very techni-cal," he said. "When I was coming up was when midi was being invented and you had to start to understand the technology as a synthesizer player – all of that in a very literal way got me gigs. I would attribute 90% of my career to my background in music.

"My life would not be nearly as rich had it not been for music. That's a certainty for me."

Park Howell, President/Owner & Pianist
President, Park & Company advertising agency
Pianist

"It [music] influentially helps you identify with something outside of your regular day-to-day world. It gives you a place to go for different perspectives on what the job may be at hand. Without it, I would feel as though I were at least a third diminished in my capabilities to do other things well."

* * *

"When they strip out music, when they strip out arts, they're stripping out the things in my mind that make us all human. Everything else is so cold; it's so binary. It's on/off. One plus one equals two. You write a sentence this way. The arts is the thread that runs through it all… It's the softer side of life."

Park Howell is the President of Park & Company in Phoenix, AZ, an integrated advertising company utilizing all forms of convergent media to facilitate their client's objectives. Park grew up in the Seattle area and received a degree from Washington State University in communications and journalism, though he also managed to complete a degree in music and theory simultaneously. He worked for a couple of different advertising agencies and as the internal creative director for a large corporation before starting his own firm in 1995.

The firm received an Emmy award (pictured above) for a television campaign that they produced for Goodwill of Central Arizona, a campaign that facilitated the client's retail sales growth from $17 million to $60 million in a six year span.

All of the subjects interviewed for this book share a passion for music and the impact that it has on business success, but Park is taking that concept to the next level.

"We just renovated our offices here with very much of a music bent," he explained gleefully. "We put in our 'creative garage' as we call it. It works for concepting, but also gives us a place to put our instruments. We have a guitar teacher who's now working with our folks. I've got a piano in my office.

"Music to me has always been not only a big part of my life, but a big part of how we communicate, because you can see the rhythms and the ebb and flow in the written word of a 30-second commercial and a well-produced brochure just like you can in the sonata form."

With the origins of his company consisting of a one-man shop with an assist from his wife, Park now has 18 full-time employees (or band members).

Park's instrument of choice has always been the piano, and those seeds were planted at a very early age.

"I was maybe five or six. My grandma and grandpa lived out in North Dakota," he recalled. "I was one of seven kids and my dad would put us all in the station wagon. We'd drive across Idaho and Montana and on into North Dakota, and we'd spend a couple of weeks in Minnesota.

"I remember standing by her side as she sat down at this old upright [piano], and she was playing 'Darktown Strutters' Ball,'" he recalled fondly. "I only know the name after the fact, but I remember her playing the song, and it's as vivid to me as anything. I remember marveling, 'How could a person get that sound out of that big black box?' And I was hooked at that point."

Park was fortunate enough to grow up in an age when pop music was heavily influenced by piano-centric recording artists. He cites Elton John as his first influence in rock/pop music. The first album he bought and the first concert he attended were Elton John recordings and performances, respectively. He also considers Queen and Freddie Mercury, Billy Joel, and the Ben Folds Five from the younger generation as influences. And from the classical side, Mozart tops his list.

Park recalled another defining moment in his musical development where the significance of music in his life rose to another level. In the ninth grade he started hanging out with his buddies and letting music slide.

He said, "I remember riding home from my paper route, and my mom stopped me and she said, 'You know Park, if you're not going to maintain your piano [studies] and keep practicing, then we're not going to keep paying for it. So you have to make a decision right now – are you going to keep playing or are you not?' It occurred to me at that point – if I stopped right then, I would never do it again and I'd probably forever miss it. So I said, 'I'm game.' I became president of the choir at the high school, accompanying them. I really dove into it."

He also remembered a music teacher, Mr. Behrens, who played a pivotal role.

[In high school] "I had this froggy voice," said Park. "It was raspy, especially when I went through puberty. It was this God-awful singing voice, and I knew it. I went in and auditioned for the choir at the prompting of my mom, so I could get in there and play some more piano and accompaniment. It was the most humiliating thing I had ever done. I know I must have sounded like the kid from The Little Rascals (referring to the character "Alfalfa" from the old television show). And he looked at me and he had nothing but great things to say."

Although Park knew the teacher was lying, it still made him feel good. To this day he still remembers what his teacher said: "You have a terrific voice, and we could use you as a baritone and as it changes maybe as a bass. I would really like you to sign up tomorrow for this." His words made Park feel like a million bucks.

Mr. Behrens also developed a composition course that he offered for one semester, simply because Park expressed an interest in it. "It was awesome," he said with affection. "The people that were in it loved it. There were five poets and five composers. It was just a high school teacher giving a damn."

Park conjectured that his life could have taken an unfavorable turn without music in the mix, indicating that he might have been an "absolute out of control hellion." He explained that he fraternized with some "fun" friends who had a propensity for trouble, and needed a constructive outlet.

"It [music] taught me determination," he said. "It gave me discipline that I would not have normally had. Being the fifth of seven kids gave me a lot of freedom to get in trouble. It kept me focused."

Given the influential role that music played in his upbringing, Park maintains strong sentiments toward the funding of the arts.

"When they strip out music, when they strip out arts, they're stripping out the things in my mind that make us all human," he said. "Everything else is so cold; it's so binary. It's on/off. One plus one equals two. You write a sentence this way.

"The arts is the thread that runs through it all. It's the softer side of Sears; remember that commercial? Sears sells all the equipment and tools, but we also have these wonderful fabrics. It's the softer side of life.

"Reading, writing, and arithmetic – that is the operational side of life," he explained. "That is the pragmatic. It's a little like a car without a really nice body and a really nice interior. It's a mode of transportation. A lawn mower is a mode of transportation. But a Ferrari can do it with so much more panache."

Park expressed three primary takeaways from music that he feels transcend the arts into the world of business.

"First and foremost, number one is discipline. It teaches you, whether you like it or not, you've got to show up every day and do it. And the more you do it, the better you get at it. That without question is the first takeaway from being involved in music.

"Number two is being able to recognize the ebb and flow of communications, particularly in my world," he indicated. "You really notice it if you sit down and study the sonata formats, and how much the sonata format mimics the world around us. It's really quite remarkable. There's a whole new appreciation for the ebb and flow of life, everything from the arts side of it to what happens on a day-to-day basis. And you've got to have the good and the bad, the minor and the major."

His third takeaway relates to the ability to look at things with a different perspective. "It also influentially helps you identify with something outside of your regular day-to-day world," he said. "It gives you a place to go for different perspectives on what the job may be at hand. Without it, I would feel as though I were at least a third diminished in my capabilities to do other things well."

By bringing music into the workplace in the literal sense, Park hopes to instill that capacity to see life and its challenges from a broader perspective in his employees, and perhaps even his clients and vendors as well.

"[Music] gives them the permission to step out of their office and try things that they haven't tried before or always wanted to try before, or to say, 'It's okay to sing in your office,'" he said insightfully. "Just to break the mold of what you would expect from a company. My big goal would be as we expand on these music lessons, I would like to offer them up to some of these kids around here that I know are coming from some of these troubled families. It just exposes more people to more things."

Park has an upright piano in his office, and visitors take notice. "It's a visual stopping point for clients, vendors, and employees," he said. 'Wow, you've got a piano in here.' It just kind of helps shake them out of their old paradigm. You don't have to lead a boring life, even at the office. Surround yourself with the stuff you love."

In retrospect, Park hypothesized that perhaps the piano idea came from the old *Dick Van Dyke* television show, of which he was a fan. As writers of a variety show, the characters portrayed by Morey Amsterdam, Rose Marie, and Dick Van Dyke always had the piano in the office to facilitate creativity.

And he closed with a few thoughts on the parallels of creativity in music and in business. "[At the piano] I just start playing randomly, not even thinking through what I'm doing," he said. "Once I feel comfortable in that zone, then I completely turn it over to the subconscious. I feel the creativity before I emit anything to paper. I don't know how to explain it.

"The closest identification would be some of these authors that are writing fiction and they say the character develops a voice of their own," he explained. "And they're just the instrument to put it down on paper. That's the best way that I can explain how I go about it.

"But it is way more subjective and intuitive than it is pragmatic," he explained. "Maybe that's full circle of this conversation on why you don't want to eliminate the arts from high school education, because everything else is pragmatic. The arts is the intuitive side. And you've got to have both to be any good at anything."

Anthony Dominici, TV Executive Producer & Guitarist

Executive Producer, ABC's *Extreme Makeover: Home Edition*,
2-time Emmy Award Winner
Guitarist

"I look back to all of those experiences that I have, being from New Orleans and appreciating these art forms – photography, visual arts, and music. Having an appreciation and a working knowledge of the history of music and jazz and pop music and pop culture – that makes what I do every day easier, because that's in my vocabulary."

* * *

"It's about storytelling. A song is a story in many ways, whether it's the emotional part of what you're listening to in a song – strings sound this way, a big bass sounds this way, and a tuba sounds this way. It's all telling a story. Whether it's the lyrics or the content of the music or the styles of the music, it's all part of how music influences what I do every day at work."

Anthony Dominici is the Executive Producer of ABC's hit television show *Extreme Makeover: Home Edition*. He served in the same capacity for *America's Next Top Model* with Tyra Banks, produced and directed variations of MTV's *The Real World*, and won two Emmy awards for his work as supervising producer of *The Amazing Race*.

He began his career as a camera assistant, learning from such masters of film as Steven Spielberg, John Woo, and Bill Condon. He graduated from the *American Film Institute* (AFI) conservatory with an MFA in Directing and a Certificate in Cinematography. He is a native of New Orleans, where he received his Bachelor of Arts in Fine Arts Photography from the *University of New Orleans*. He also attended the *New Orleans Center for Creative Arts* (NOCCA), an intensive arts training program for gifted secondary school-aged students.

Anthony started our conversation by briefly discussing his transition from making over models to making over homes. "It's pretty interesting for sure," Anthony remarked. "It's a bigger endeavor, but it's been a lot of fun and quite a learning experience. When I worked on *The Real World*, we would go and 'build' a house, meaning outfit it with cameras wherever we would rent a place. And we did the same thing with *America's Next Top Model* to a much smaller extent.

"We're literally going in, tearing down a house, and 106 hours later moving a family into the new house that's completely outfitted, down to the clothes in the closet," said Anthony of his new challenge. "That's pretty intense, pretty awesome, I must say. I feel lucky to work on a show like this. You really are making peoples' lives better by what we're doing every day. We're finding people who are not only in need, but who are deserving of that help. I consider myself a very small cog in the wheel compared to many others who are actually swinging hammers and doing literally the heavy lifting. I'm just a guy who's making a TV show about that."

Anthony was very humble regarding his accomplishments, yet he has achieved tremendous success in a highly competitive business. In terms of advice for other aspiring filmmakers and those pursuing any artistic profession, his recommendation was simple.

"Choose a career that you want to do," he said plainly. "I don't consider my job a job. Yes, I have to work hard and travel a lot, and I work long hours, probably 17-hour days. What I do is an extension of who I am as a person. Whether it's playing music or creating stories or creating television or writing a script or whatever. That's all who I am, and I don't want to turn that off. I'm trying to perfect myself as an artist and reach my own goals as an artist by doing that. Try to find a career where you can do what you love and get paid to do it."

Anthony spoke of his participation in the unique program at NOCCA, clearly a defining time in his development as a person and as an artist. "NOCCA was truly a life changing experience in my life," he said. "I'd gone to Catholic schools for high school and grammar school before. It was definitely a good education and everything, but there was definitely something lacking in terms of being able to really artistically express myself. In Catholic high school you're wearing quasi-military khakis, so it's not about self-expression. It's about education and stripping all of that stuff away.

"NOCCA was really eye-opening for me to see that there were other weird people like me who liked weird music, liked art, were expressive, and liked to dress maybe a little bit differently than the norm. I just didn't know that. There weren't that many people at my high school that were like that – that found a different way to express themselves."

Anthony confided that during his time at NOCCA was the first time he felt that he fit in. Being around different people whom he could relate to was definitely a positive experience.

"But also, it was a great way for a youngster to make art, to say things in a different way, and also to learn about the different kinds of processes in doing things," he said. "I learned about photography which really led to my career in the film business. I was a Visual Arts major, so it was painting, drawing, and sculpture and all of these things that I had some exposure to in my life, but nothing to the level that NOCCA provided.

"It's great that kids have an opportunity," he added. "It's such an important aspect of education. Music and the arts are as important as anything else in teaching kids how to express themselves and define a path in life that may be different than just a corporate business structure."

Having an opportunity to participate in such an esteemed and advanced program for the arts, Anthony finds it difficult to fathom the concept of an educational institution without at least some perfunctory outlet for artistic expression.

"When you hear that any public schools don't have art programs or even physical education programs, it's like, 'Wow, what are kids doing these days to express themselves?' To create a new point of view and create a new culture, that's what music does," he testified. "That's what art does. It influences the popular culture in many ways, from rock and roll to cubist art. It changes the way that people perceive the world. Without an outlet for that, it's just a real shame."

While Anthony's vocation is film, music has also played an important role in his development. A guitarist from an early age, he has been influenced as much by the musical culture that is such an integral part of New Orleans as he has been by playing music.

"I play guitar and used to play in some rock bands in New Orleans," he said. "I still play every day. On the crew of *Extreme Makeover: Home Edition*, there are a couple of guys who get together and have jam sessions. We play concerts and do little fund raisers as sort of an extra-curricular activity because we're on the road so much. It is also a great expressive outlet."

Anthony was born and raised in New Orleans. He moved away when he was 26 years old to go to Graduate school at the AFI in Los Angeles. "I started playing guitar literally before kindergarten, taking guitar lessons," he said. "That was my opening to music at a very early age. My mom's from Cuba, and I used to love Jose Feliciano. I would play along and sing along to his music. That was literally my first exposure to it. So I wanted to play guitar. I didn't keep with the lessons, so I'm not a [music notation] reader, but I can play along and figure out songs pretty quickly.

"In my personal life, it's [music] a very calming and soothing sort of thing," he revealed. "It keeps me very focused as well. It's a great companion to my everyday job, which is literally being the boss in charge of 200 people building a house at any given time."

Anthony expressed the effect of music in terms of its unique impact on his artistic perspective on the totality of life.

"I listen to New Orleans music literally every day of my life, from James Booker to the Nevilles to the Meters," he said proudly. "Being from New Orleans, that's who I am. I'm sure most people from New Orleans would probably say the same thing, but it's such an engrained part of who I am as a person and everything that I know and love and enjoy and appreciate about music and art and culture and architecture and everything. New Orleans was such a unique place to grow up. That has absolutely influenced everything that I do down to the words that I choose, how I say them, my personality, and my whole approach to life."

Anthony's approach to fervently participating in and enjoying the experience of life carries over into his work. "My whole approach to running crews on a reality show is like, 'Look, yes it's hard work. We have to sort of trudge through the tough stuff. But if we're not having fun at it, then why are we doing it? Why do we do this at all if we're not having fun?'" he said.

Being the Executive Producer of a television show, Anthony's musical foundation provides a more tangible benefit when the songs used to capture the appropriate emotions of each episode are chosen.

"My mother was a painter and sculptor, and my dad was a drafting instructor at the local community college," Anthony explained. "I knew that I was good at drawing and visual arts. I knew that I enjoyed playing music. For me being a visual artist, filmmaking and making television truly put that all together.

What the pictures should look like from the photography, but also what are the emotions when we're editing the show. Saying, 'Oh, this music doesn't work because it's too crazy or too funny and it's supposed to be a sensitive scene. So we've got to find a music cue that sounds more like this.' I give very specific direction all of the time when I'm putting together episodes of these shows.

"I look back to all of those experiences that I have, being from New Orleans and appreciating these art forms – photography, visual arts, and music," Anthony disclosed. "Having an appreciation and a working knowledge of the history of music and jazz and pop music and pop culture – that makes what I do every day easier, because that's in my vocabulary.

"It's about storytelling," he clarified. "A song is a story in many ways, whether it's the emotional part of what you're listening to in a song – strings sound this way, a big bass sounds this way, and a tuba sounds this way. It's all telling a story. Whether it's the lyrics or the content of the music or the styles of the music, it's all part of how music influences what I do every day at work."

Anthony believes that whether someone plays music or is just a fan, people can always learn something from that, because music gets your mind going to places where you might not get to on your own – whether it's experiencing an emotion or trying to express something in a certain way.

Certain songs, musicians, or albums can create place marks that help us put a historical perspective and an emotional context on our lives, a concept that Anthony refers to as "scoring your life with music that you love." He candidly shared a story from his own recent past that illustrated that point.

"Months after Hurricane Katrina, my folks still lived in New Orleans and we tried to rescue as much as we could," Anthony said, referring to the damaged possessions ravaged by the flooding. "I'd taken all of these old photos that had turned to just 'muck,' and tried to save them. I happened to be listening to Fats Domino's 'Walking to New Orleans.' I'd heard the song a thousand times, and it never moved me until I'm sitting there thinking about home and listening to this guy singing about walking to New Orleans because New Orleans is my home.

"Whether you're creating your own story or using music to sort of score your story and to inspire your own life, it is such an important outlet. I don't think there's really five minutes in the day where I'm not listening to music or getting inspired by it in some way or another. Whether it's a tone or a mood or a thought or a feeling, it's so necessary."

It was only fitting that since Anthony's connection to music is inextricable from the city in which he grew up that his final thoughts drifted back to New Orleans.

"It's such a beautiful thing to have a city that's so rich in its own culture," he said sincerely. "I feel so lucky to be from there. It has absolutely influenced and created who I am as a person, as an artist, and even as a business person. It's an attitude that I convey that has been a part of my success."

Bob Knott, Executive Vice-President & Guitarist
Executive Vice-President, Edelman, global independent public relations firm
Guitarist, Music Critic

"For me creativity is like being in a band. In five minutes, I'm going to walk into a room to talk about a multi-million dollar RFP (Request for Proposal). I'm going to go in there with an idea or two or three or four, and I'm going to sit down with other senior people in the firm. As if we were a jazz combo, we're going to just start riffing off of one another, and we're going to find a rhythm – a creative, strategic rhythm. And then we're going to come out with some really good ideas."

* * *

"I don't want to belabor the parallel, but when you have people who speak the same language, musical language or intellectual language, people who have similar skill sets and traits and talents, and you bring them together with a common purpose, good things often happen."

Bob Knott is an Executive Vice-President and U.S. Practice Head for Edelman, one of the leading global independent public relations firms. The award-winning firm has 3,100 employees in 51 offices, and Bob is a Baltimore native working in the firm's Washington, D.C. office. He joined the firm nine years ago and considers it one of the best decisions he's ever made.

Edelman once again has garnered its share of the industry's top honors in 2009, recognizing among other accomplishments the firm's continued robust growth. The Edelman client list includes Heinz, Wyeth, Butterball, Johnson & Johnson, UPS, and Kraft.

Bob has always considered himself a music junkie, boasting more than 20,000 songs on his iPod. Even before playing an instrument and performing became a significant part of his life, the experience of enjoying music left an indelible impression on him. He recalled his early memories of music with remarkable clarity.

"My father was an unrepentant music junkie," Bob said. "When I was a very young boy, as young as four or five, my father would go for hours at a time and shop for vinyl records. I remember going to the music store and listening to The Allman Brothers, Janis Joplin, Otis Redding, and all of this great timeless music piped in overhead. I remember flipping through the great big album cover artwork. I remember looking at the (Rolling) Stones' *Sticky Fingers* album and actually seeing an operating zipper on the cover. I'd look at the visual and hear the music.

"On one such excursion my father bought me two albums, *The Jackson Five's Greatest Hits* and the Beatles' Blue Album (*The Beatles/1967-1970*) – the double compilation album of the latter years of their career," Bob fondly recalled. "I remember not long ago recounting that experience with my father. I remember that day so clearly. Most kids, if they had any exposure to or appreciation for music, were listening to the Mickey Mouse Club or something similar."

Bob's appreciation for music is what defines him as a person. And although he has an incredibly diverse music library, there are a few artists that have left a more prominent impression, for various reasons.

"Bob Dylan, Radiohead, Hendrix, The Rolling Stones' *Sticky Fingers* album," Bob responded to my inquiry regarding those artists that uniquely speak to him. "It's [*Sticky Fingers*] an album that means a lot to me for a lot of reasons. When I was a kid, my mother died. I was barely twelve years old. That just sucks.

Music was a place where I could go. I'm uncomfortable saying it's a place where I retreated, but it just made life a lot better. I really focused on the Stones at a time when having that place to go to was a really good thing. So for personal reasons I got turned on to the Stones at an important time in my life.

"But also, separately, *Sticky Fingers* is my favorite album of all time," Bob remarked, referring to the purely artistic merits of the recording. "In my estimation, there's not a single album that better demonstrates the breadth of rock and roll. [Elements of] Straight-up rock, jazz, country, blues, and even the use of strings. No one album so deftly spans all of the influences that constitute the stew that is rock and roll. And clearly, the Stones were at the height of their powers then."

Bob recalled having a guitar around the house as a youngster, but it wasn't until much later that he seriously pursued the instrument.

"I got a guitar when I was in grade school, probably seventh or eighth grade, an acoustic guitar," Bob said. "But I wasn't really serious about it. After graduating high school, I bought an electric guitar and really focused on it. Whereas before the guitar had been an accessory, something to lean against the wall in my bedroom, I now looked at it not just as an instrument but a creative outlet – as a way to make real the creative ideas that I had – and therefore I became increasingly focused on it.

"And I actually got pretty good," he added. "I could within reason, hear something and figure out how to play it, despite never having had a lesson – despite really having no formal grasp of music theory or even knowing the notes that I was playing. I wound up playing bands and somebody would say, 'Play a 'B' or this chord progression or this type of scale.' To this day I have completely no concept of what they're talking about. Do I know the names of maybe five or six chords? Sure. I've nevertheless been able to pick up the instrument and figure it out."

I was intrigued by the fact that the guitar was readily available to Bob, yet didn't become a significant outlet for him until years later. Often musicians can point to defining moments when their interest in music elevated to another level. For Bob, it seems as though he had reached an introspective point in his life when he lacked direction. As we've discussed previously, music and the arts can serve as an invaluable catalyst in an individual's journey of discovery. The guitar seems to have filled precisely that role for Bob.

"I took a couple of years off after graduating high school before going to college," Bob explained. "I think for me the guitar became an outlet, absent anything else substantive in my life. When you stop going to school for the first time in your life since you were a child, you have a job but not a career. The guitar constituted something purposeful. It allowed me to channel creative and even intellectual energies in a place that was somewhat productive. It was at that point that I actually began to focus on it, and I actually had more time.

"In a very conventional sense, I was going nowhere fast," Bob recounted. "I was saving money to go to college and do other things. I was really able to focus on music and what I was listening to. And then to some meaningful extent, I was able to translate it and make what I was always listening to real in my life by playing guitar."

Bob is another one of the research participants who was able to garner self-esteem from the music experience and who seemed unable to find that level of substantiation in other pursuits.

"There are a lot of very smart people who, for whatever reason, are square pegs trying to fit into a round hole. The arts and music in particular is a path forward for people," he concluded based on his experience. Bob characterized himself as one of those square pegs.

"I've written on behalf of Fortune 500 companies while at large firms, and I've been published as a freelance writer," he noted. "I'm good at what I do, and one of the things that I do is write. I remember handing in a really good paper, and a teacher at a very expensive prep school saying, 'You didn't write this.' I just remember feeling really lousy about myself. But music for me was something that I knew was good at, because people I really admired were playing that, and I was able to play that same thing. For me it provided a level of validation and affirmation that I had really never gotten in most other places in my life."

Bob's thoughts then turned to the importance of music in a broader context.

"Music transcends culture," he said. "It transcends any and all barriers, be they socio-economic, be they cultural, be they geographic. There is something primal about music. It's essential to the human condition. It's been there forever. As long as there has been man, there has been music. To cultivate something that is essential to the human condition is – well – essential.

"Secondly, I find music to be critical, certainly in an educational environment. History is replete with very, very bright people who, for whatever reason don't conform and don't measure up to the standard metrics for success, be they academic or societal. Music has nevertheless allowed people to express themselves and to contribute to society and to make art. It's an opportunity for people who don't have a lot of opportunities in the conventional sense.

"History is bursting with artists pursuing art after having been rejected in some fashion or underestimated by the conventional rules. Art and music in particular is every bit as essential as reading, writing, and 'rithmetic."

Bob has also found that bringing music into the workplace in the literal sense can have its advantages.

"It's difficult to overstate but it is nevertheless overlooked commonly, the influence environment has on one's professional output, on one's work," Bob noted. "We need to think creatively and strategically. For me at least, I need to do that in an environment that's conducive to thinking that way. So here in my office, I have limited edition photographic prints. I've got Keith Richards there, Hendrix there, Cobain here, Patti Smith there, Elvis Presley there. I've got a couple of albums signed by Wilco over here.

"I was in here at 7:15 this morning cranking up David Bowie on my iPod really loud before everyone else showed up," he added. "For me that's a very creative, charged atmosphere. And for me, I like that. I'm able to think better that way. I can't write when I'm listening to NPR, but I can write when I'm listening to Bob Dylan. There's something about the environment that changes when I've got music on or when I'm surrounded by music. And it [the type of music] changes. It's usually reflective of my mood."

For some, the capacity for creativity and innovation can be enhanced by finding the right collaborator (or collaborators). Bob discussed that concept in the context of public relations work, drawing the parallels to his experience playing in a band.

"When I played in a band I worked in the context of a team," Bob stated. "Now at one of the world's largest agencies I have a role to play, but I do so in the context of a team. Music and the business that I'm in, marketing and communications broadly defined, there's a relationship. They're subjective in nature. There is something subjective and creative and free-flowing about music, and there's something subjective, creative, and free-flowing about marketing and communications. The two are linked.

"Just as one person in a band does not at the end of the day do all of the work, in my business one person doesn't have all of the answers," Bob acknowledged. "I'm only as good as my team in a band, and likewise I'm just as good as my team in public relations.

"For me creativity is like being in a band," he explained. "In five minutes, I'm going to walk into a room to talk about a multi-million dollar RFP (Request for Proposal). And I'm going to go in there with an idea or two or three or four, and I'm going to sit down with other senior people in the firm. As if we were a jazz combo, we're going to just start riffing off of one another, and we're going to find a rhythm, a creative, strategic rhythm. And then we're going to come out with some really good ideas.

"I don't want to belabor the parallel, but when you have people who speak the same language, musical language or intellectual language, people who have similar skill sets and traits and talents, and you bring them together with a common purpose, good things often happen. You find a creative rhythm and strategic rhythm in both the musical and business contexts."

Bob addressed the concept of taking risks in the pursuit of creative breakthroughs, a certain necessity in his line of work.

"You can only say the same thing once and truly be creative while saying it the first time," Bob suggested. "I can play a guitar solo, and it will never be more creative than the first time I played it. And the more I play it, the less creative it will be. Obviously, the same is true of business. Somebody's not paying my hourly rate if I'm coming up with the same old ideas. Improvisationally, which is to say in a meeting or when I'm sitting in my office thinking big thoughts with my team, you have to swing for the fences in terms of what we recommend to the client and what we execute.

"You have to take a chance, and you have to sort of break ground that has often never been broken before, at least with the client," he added. "In public relations in particular, people are coming to this because they have more questions than answers, and you have to tell them to do something that they're not accustomed to doing. And you really do have to swim against the current. You have to tell them something often times that they don't want to accept and worse still, don't want to do.

"There is an inherent measure of risk in what I do, because you have to step out," Bob said. "For you to distinguish yourself from other firms and others who do what you do, you need to think differently. If you look at the great artists of our time, they broke new ground. They did what nobody else did before. And they never would have accomplished that unless they took risks.

"And likewise the people who are the true pioneers in any industry are the people who took risks. By definition, if it's never been done before, there wasn't a market for it, and there wasn't necessarily a need for it. A popular business euphemism based on a quote from hockey player Wayne Gretzky who said that success for him was going to where the puck was going to be, not where it was. If you look at the champions of commerce – Henry Ford. He didn't just come up with a car everybody was going to like; he came up with the assembly line, which gave birth to the industrial age. He did something different, and then everybody followed him."

Bob once again turned to music icons to further illustrate his point. "I heard something about Dylan which defined in part his genius," he said. "People came to Dylan. By the time people started to figure out Dylan and go where he was, he'd move. He'd pick up camp and he'd move. I think the relationship between risk and music and commerce are inextricable and they are completely related. Nobody ever played the guitar like Hendrix – then or now – the way he did."

And Bob closed by articulating the important role that music education can play in cultivating that individuality, which can foster those unconventional, pioneering ideas.

"The value of music especially in the context of education – it's where the music can conform to an individual's talents, whereas in typical standardized testing formats, the individual has to conform to the conventional standards," he said. "That's a nice switch. A kid can rise up and be looked upon as great or talented or special. The best artists almost by definition are not conventional. So often in an educational environment, be it public or private you're held to largely conventional standards and norms."

Rodger Roeser, President/G.M.
& Bass Guitarist/Singer
President & General Manager, Eisen
Management Group, public relations firm
Former Bass Guitarist/Lead Singer of Turning Force

"For me it [the greatest benefit of music] was that confidence in my creativity. I felt comfortable that when I would write a song, I felt as though with some tweaking, 'Hey, this is a pretty good song. I can write.'"

* * *

"I think going out there and putting that in front of people – I do that every day in my real job. I'm creating ads. I'm developing releases. I'm developing campaigns and marketing programs. And I've not only got to take that to my clientele to look at, to approve, and to understand my vision. But I'm also taking that to consumers for them to absorb, for them to see, and for them to acknowledge whether this is good or bad."

Rodger Roeser is the president of an integrated buzz marketing, social media, and public relations firm, Eisen Management Group. The company is headquartered in Cleveland, Ohio, with branch offices in Greater Cincinnati. He is the former Vice President of Justice & Young Advertising and Public Relations, former Senior Consultant with HSR Business to Business, and the former General Manager of VMS Ohio. He is an award winning newspaper reporter and editor with the Lorain Morning Journal and Bellevue Gazette Company, and former news anchor and reporter for TV2News and WCPZ102.7FM.

Yet music actually provided the foundation for everything that Rodger has achieved in the field of public relations. As a member of the band Turning Force he took control of the business aspects of touring and promotion, and the band scored a *Billboard* Top 100 hit and an MTV video in 1990 with "Was It You," a song Rodger refers to as a "hair band ballad."

Rodger grew up on a farm, far removed from the world of rock and roll. His first memory of music was singing "Delta Dawn" for a local talent contest in a town of 600. The introduction to the rock band KISS by an older cousin expanded his view of the possibilities of music.

"As an impressionable young boy, you look at these posters and you look at this stuff and you say, 'Wow, that's kinda cool.' It really changed my perception of music," he recalled. "I remember getting my first KISS eight-track [tape]. It was an album called *Double Platinum*. It was like a greatest hits album in 1978. I just listened to that thing like crazy. I became a huge fan. I wanted to be in KISS.

"I would do make-up and I would sing songs," he added. "I didn't know how to play guitar. I didn't know how to do any of that, but I could sing. I was probably eight or nine years old, and I'm writing my own songs. My parents have old eight-millimeter [film] of me singing into a pretend microphone. That's how that came about."

Rodger recalled singing in the choir in school and playing the lead in all of the high school musicals. He characterized the experience as something that he really enjoyed, though the material he had to work with was perhaps less than stellar. "One [of the musicals] was *Let George Do It*, which was a biography of George Washington, and I played George," Rodger said. "The other one was called *Teen*. I even remember one of the songs, which is terrifying," he said with amusement.

Rodger recalled forming a band at the age of twelve. "My best friend [Mark] who I've known since kindergarten started playing guitar and his older brother [Joe] played piano," Rodger said. "I could sing so I said, 'Let's form a band.' And we did. I mean we were horrible. I had written some songs, and of course they're terrible. We were driving our parents crazy and playing in every garage that we could. This is when it's fortunate that you live out in the middle of nowhere, because your material's loud and it sucks.

"We were called Reaction, which is a great name for that band, because I'm sure we gave people a reaction," he said jokingly. "I remember our first gig. I was 13 and we were playing on the back of a semi truck bed in a town called Fremont, Ohio at the sauerkraut festival or something like that. We had no equipment, we were horrifically bad, and we played outside on a truck bed. There's nothing worse than a 13-year-old boy singing 'Rock You Like a Hurricane' by the Scorpions."

Rodger insisted that they gave it their all and didn't let their detractors get them down. They began to build a repertoire of pop songs of the day by artists such as The Cars, Loverboy, and Bryan Adams, occasionally venturing into harder rock material, though they were limited by their abilities. To this point, the story of Rodger's band mimics that of thousands of garage bands. It was their unwavering focus and resolve that brought success to Rodger and his band mates.

"When I went to college, that's when I started playing guitar, 'cause we needed a bass player and we couldn't find one," he noted. "I would not consider myself naturally musically inclined. As far as a rock voice goes, I have a really good singing voice, but I never considered myself a musician.

"Mark had the patience of Job, and he'd sit down and literally note by note teach me how to play [bass] guitar," Rodger added. "While everybody was out boozing it up, we were practicing guitar, practicing singing, and practicing harmonizing. We were doing all the things that we possibly could to get better.

"We literally just practiced all the time," he said, underscoring their steadfast commitment to music. "I mean all the time. I practiced constantly on my own, working out the bass and learning material. All of this time we were writing, and we had written several songs that we thought were pretty good."

The band's first venture into the studio turned out to be a learning experience, though the results didn't quite live up to expectations. "At this point is when we wrote 'Was It You' in 1989," Rodger recalled. "We had gone into a local studio and recorded it, and the recording was just terrible. We didn't know what to expect. We didn't really understand it. Certainly we weren't terribly talented. But we went in and recorded a demo and were shopping it around. And it was nice to have a demo, because it was at least good enough to send out to the clubs and bars."

Most every successful band goes through a period of maturity during which the challenge of playing a regular schedule of lackluster venues hones their skills. The Beatles played an exhausting schedule of club dates in Hamburg and Liverpool before becoming an "overnight success" in America. And with a demo tape in hand, Rodger and his cronies, now performing under the name Turning Force, were able to book a consistent schedule of live dates that sharpened their skills.

"We were playing at least two to three times a month, college bars and festivals," Rodger said. "That's really when you started to get good. You're actually performing this material live. The gigs were four hours long. You would play from 10 [p.m.] until 2 [a.m.]. We would pepper in the originals as we could. That was our college job. We're honing our skills. We're getting much better at it.

"It's like exercise," he added. "Our shows were intense. We're plucking our guitars, jumping around, pointing at girls, and all this other stuff. We've got lights bearing down on us, and the guitar weighs about 20 pounds. We were all in fantastic shape. You bring in all this equipment, and then after the show was over, you tear it all down. We're fortunate that we were young, because I couldn't do that now. It was intense."

With a little bit more seasoning, the band returned to the studio, and this time the experience and the results were quite different.

"It was 1990," Rodger remembered. "We went into the studio. By this point we were a pretty decent band. We went in and recorded a single called 'Give in to Me' which was maybe the fifth or sixth original song we had written. We went to a really nice studio with a really good guy. He really understood what we were trying to do, and we produced a hit. We were like 'Wow, this is cool.'"

The popularity of that recording brought the band a certain level of celebrity and success.

"We sent it to all the radio stations in Cleveland, and one of the stations put it into the regular rotation and played it all the time. Then we were renting out theaters. We were renting out the State Theater, the Town and Country Theater. We're renting out big clubs and selling our own tickets.

"And that's really when I think things exploded," Rodger added. "Then I'm promoting the band. We've got this song on the radio. That's pretty cool. You're driving down the street and your song comes on. We were doing well. Thousands and thousands of cassette tapes of that single were done. From there we performed every dirtball club from Detroit to Pittsburgh and everywhere in between all along the golden crescent of Lake Erie."

It was out of necessity based upon the burgeoning success of the band that Rodger began to shoulder the business aspects of handling a successful rock and roll band. All of the elements of band and show promotion would have a very direct correlation with success in his eventual career path.

"We were doing our thing and then obviously we had a big hit in '92 with 'Was It You,'" said Rodger of the band's *Billboard* Top 100 hit. "For us it was a big hit. It was all of the work in planning the event, promoting the shows, sending out press kits, reaching out to media folks, pitching the band, getting stories, publicizing the programs, making videos, and going to the studio – through trial by fire, I learned how to be a pretty damned good P.R. guy.

"I wouldn't say that I knew what the hell I was doing," he admitted. "I probably made more mistakes than any human being should be allowed to have. You learn from those, you grow from those, and you become better at it. At the heyday of our live performances, we were doing three, four, five, six, seven, or eight shows a week."

The band continued to pursue their dream, even while holding down regular day jobs.

"I remember I was the P.R. director at a company up in Cleveland," Rodger said of his hectic schedule. "I would literally go from my suit and tie in the afternoon and change into my leather pants at the office to get to the gig on time to set stuff up. And all of us were like that. I'm working in P.R., and Mark is working as an engineer. It was not uncommon for us to have 24 hour days. And again, I could never do that now. But when you're 25, 26, 27 years old, you say, 'Whatever.'"

Rodger and his band mates had a laser-like focus on their dream, an attribute that steered them clear of the trappings that so often derail aspiring musicians. "You have to understand that while being a musician is all fun, it's a business," he said with conviction. "There's no time to get stoned. There's no time to be getting drunk. There's no time for any of this nonsense. You've got a job to do. I saw people around us who would get high, and we never did any of that. Never. Too smart for it. That's just such an easy downward spiral to get into."

Rodger articulated the most prominent benefit from music in terms of his business success. "For me it was that confidence in my creativity," he said. "I felt comfortable that when I would write a song, that I felt as though with some tweaking, 'Hey, this is a pretty good song. I can write.' I think going out there and putting that in front of people – I do that every day in my real job. I'm creating ads. I'm developing releases. I'm developing campaigns and marketing programs. And I've not only got to take that to my clientele to look at, to approve, and to understand my vision, but I'm also taking that to consumers for them to absorb, for them to see, and for them to acknowledge whether this is good or bad.

"Music taught me more than just music," he added. "Anybody can do Es or Ds or Fs and all that other stuff. To me that's not what music was all about. To me music was about establishing that outlet for an only child to have an incredible amount of creativity, but also to put that creativity and channel it in a very good and positive way. Not through some video game called Rock Star or Rock Band. And to get out there and experience all of that. It's translated to and permeated through my entire life."

The experience of performing live on stage in front of thousands of fans also gave Rodger a sense of assuredness that has carried forward to business and an understanding that preparation is the only authentic source of that assuredness.

"Confidence comes from practicing your ass off and knowing that you're going to go up there on stage, or in business that you're going to go up there for your presentation and kick ass. That's where confidence comes from. Otherwise, you just have false confidence or you're a braggart."

Creating material and a musical experience that address the demands of music audiences has really given Rodger a valuable perspective on customer service too.

"For me, it's really about understanding who you're speaking to and what it is you're trying to say to them," he explained. "You've got to get outside of yourself, and you've got to think about what it is that other people around you are seeing, hearing, or witnessing. How best to see those things around you and convey those things in such a way that they go, 'Hmmm, that's cool' or 'That's an interesting perspective I may not have thought about.'

"We've got songs that run the gamut from 'Gee, I really love you and I'm sad that you broke up with me' to songs that are really politically based to songs that are, 'We need to be paying attention to what the hell's going on in the world and be smarter about things,'" he explained.

"To me it's [songwriting] all about introspection and allegory. And I think if more people can put themselves in other people's minds and other people's shoes, this would be a much better world."

He also equates having a great song to having a great product or a great invention. "You've got to market that, you've got to get it into the hands of the right people, you've got to be lucky, and you've got to be tenacious," he said. "You've got to have a lot of 'stick-to-itiveness' and gastric fortitude, for lack of a better term."

Building something successful from the ground up also provided a foundation for Rodger to lead a business. "I think it really drove my entrepreneurial spirit," he stated confidently. "And if it's taught me anything – nothing comes easy. I can tell you many a night when we would lug up speakers and amps and guitars and lights and fog and lasers and bust our ass to please drunk people in an audience. It teaches you a lot of humility. It teaches you you're going to have to play a lot of hole in the wall clubs before you're doing anything that's going to make a difference.

"To me that's a big lesson," he explained. "There are so many people who expect it to be handed to them. They're just so good, or they're just so smart that they're entitled to it. I've never discovered anything that replaced good, hard work."

Growing up in a small rural town, music became a positive vehicle that really expanded the options in life for Rodger. He speculated that his future would have consisted of working in factory or on a farm, if music would not have opened up a whole new world of possibilities. As a result, he feels strongly that other kids should have the same exposure to music that was afforded him.

"You can either stick a guitar or a piano in some people's hands, or you can stick some pot or some pills or some cigarettes or some booze. Let me know which one is going to reap long term rewards," he said passionately, "because they both kill time beautifully. So which one do you want your kids to be exposed to? Which one is actually going to be a creative outlet? Because kids by definition are creative, they're curious. Hell of a lot easier, trust me, to learn how to play guitar or piano when you're seven than when you're seventeen. It was like learning a new language for me. Our schools need less Ritalin and more guitars."

And even a less than positive experience in music can provide a valuable learning experience, according to Rodger. "Music allows you to learn how to fail," he concluded. "To learn how to go out there and put yourself on the line and realize that not everybody's going to love you. Not everybody's going to tell you how wonderful you are. Typically it's the people that come to you and say, 'This really sucks, you need to step it up' that you learn from the most."

SECTION III

Music &
My Business

*Professionals for Whom Music
Is a Part of Their Business*

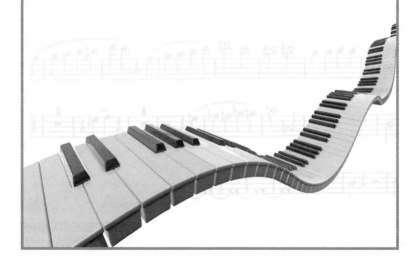

Dr. Michael Gold, Founding Principal & Upright Bass Player
The Jazz Impact Workshop
(Parallels from the world of business illustrated through jazz improvisation)
Upright Bass player, Music Educator

"What's going on in jazz is that we are constantly taking the risk of prototyping new ideas. That's what improvisation means. If we want to be a culture of innovation...we have to redefine how we take risks and how we think about risk."

* * *

"We have a structure. But it's set up in such a way that enables us to constantly take the risk of trying new ideas. And when they work, they change the structure. And that changes the possibilities of what we can come up with. Risk becomes an element that is no longer a choice."

Dr. Michael Gold is founder and principal of Jazz Impact. His Jazz Impact workshops demonstrate how the dynamics of a jazz improvisational combo can teach lessons that attendees can apply to the business world. He is a musician, and former music educator, and once worked in operations for a financial services firm. The latter experience gave him an invaluable opportunity in the sense that he was able to approach many of the issues of a traditional corporate setting with the sensibilities of a musician.

Perhaps the highest compliment I can pay to Michael is that his work, including a book he was working on at the time of our initial conversation, covers much of the same ground as this one, yet he shared his insights candidly and without reservation. He is one of the most engaging and sincere people I've had the pleasure to meet, and his insights were tremendous.

Michael's first memories of music were that of his mother, a piano major in college, playing the family's Steinway baby grand. His parents had jazz records, and he came of age in the mid-60s. He also had a school orchestra that was open to students of all ages, so accessibility to music was never an issue.

Like most musicians, Michael had a breakthrough moment with respect to his musical development that he recalled with absolute clarity. "Something happened at the age of seven that totally transformed me," he recalled. "It had to do with my next door neighbor. I grew up in the Hudson Valley, about 75 miles north of New York City. These guys had one of the best bands in the New York state area, and they practiced in their garage. One day they opened the garage and there they were having this rehearsal. They later went on to sign with Mercury Records.

"I remember walking over, and all of the kids in the neighborhood came to see," he added. "I think they were playing Beach Boys songs or something. I was absolutely transfixed by the bass player. The power of the sound went right through me. From that day on I became a bass player. It was almost as if all of the experiences I had prior to that led up to the impact of that one experience."

Michael played electric bass in high school, gravitating toward blues and rock and roll at that time. Later he began to discover the allure of acoustic music and migrated to the upright bass, exploring various forms of music such as bluegrass, swing, and "old-time" bands. He discovered an intimacy in music that is acoustic or performed at lower volume, and he uses that intimacy to make his workshops a great success. He articulated that feeling, in terms of the vibe created between audience and musician.

"There was a serious energy exchange [whenever I was on stage]," he said. "Looking back on it I'm very aware of why it was such a powerful experience. At the time, I can't say that I really understood it. But I knew that the energy of the music that we were generating was being received by the people we were playing it for, and that it was coming back to us. There was a loop that was happening. It became a very compelling experience that I couldn't let go of.

"The intensity of that loop for me was greater when I was playing an acoustic instrument than when I was playing an electric instrument," he added. "I really believe that the power of jazz has to do with the fact that people are able to be in such close proximity to the real making of that music and not receiving it through the huge decibel levels that people are assaulted with in rock and roll."

Michael recalled some of the musicians and mentors that facilitated his migration toward jazz. "At a certain point, I'd say in 10th grade, somebody gave me a Charlie Parker record. It just blew my mind," he said. Michael even took up the alto sax seriously for some time.

"I saw the James Cotton Blues Band. The power that he brought to the stage, and I don't mean volume – I mean the emotional commitment that he demonstrated very deeply affected me. I really made a connection between blues and jazz, and that for me was a vehicle out of rock and roll."

The decision to explore the world of jazz was only the initial step. Michael provided insight into the discipline required to achieve a high level of artistry by conveying some of the lessons of his mentors.

"A jazz bass player by the name of Chuck Israel (Michael pointed out that Israel had played with John Coltrane and ran the National Jazz Ensemble) came to my school and did a workshop," he recalled. "He took me aside and said, 'You know, you have the potential to be a good bass player.' He gave me some Oscar Pettiford records and told me to go home and learn the solos. When I asked how he said, 'Just listen to them until you can play them.' And I did."

Michael revealed that following Israel's advice transformed everything for him, because it was almost like taking private lessons with one of the great jazz bass players. "You integrate that music – you take that music inside of you," he explained. "That experience in and of itself expanded my desire to read more and to explore other areas that I didn't really know about. It gave me an understanding of bass playing that I had been searching for and hadn't found in all of the method books."

Michael later began to study with a pianist named Sal Mosca, a protégé of Lennie Tristano. "He taught me the deep experience of ear training, the discipline of learning to sing with records, the master improvisations of all time, and learning to play what you hear as an individual rather than trying to model yourself after somebody else," he explained.

Michael earned a doctorate in jazz studies, played professionally for years, and later ran the jazz studies program at Vassar College.

If jazz improvisation is a metaphor and a lesson for introducing creativity into the workplace, then it's important to understand the philosophy that leads the musician to the discovery of new ideas. Michael noted Edward Huizenga's work (author of *Innovation Management in the ICT Sector: How Frontrunners Stay Ahead*) – the concept of play being critical for creativity.

"What I'm trying to do in jazz is constantly achieve a position of childlike approach to the process, which is very hard because I've spent thousands of hours practicing and studying, listening, forming opinions, and understanding my own creativity," he said. "And to really improvise, you have to get past all that. You have to let go of that and discover it anew.

"I think that is the key – to come at what you're doing with no expectation – to be surprised and delighted by what you're discovering. That really is the key I think."

If we think of the workplace and the business professional, the challenge ahead of us is daunting. We take ourselves so seriously in the office. We went to school and toiled for years, and possibly earned a degree or even multiple degrees. We climbed our way up the corporate ladder. We sacrificed weekends or evenings and family time, taking on added responsibilities to demonstrate our commitment. We present a certain persona in the office that we believe will create a perception of success.

Given that environment, it's hard to think of corporate America as an arena for playfulness, delight, and childlike discovery. Yet that's exactly what we must aspire to become. As Michael observed, we must let go of our preconceptions of our business, our job, and the systems that dictate our actions in the workplace, and discover them anew.

Teamwork and collaboration are lessons that translate from the music experience to the workplace. Michael understands the interconnectivity of the members of a musical combo – the realization that the action of every player has an effect on every other player, and therefore on the dynamics of the group. During his tenure as Vice-President of Operations for a financial services firm with seven locations and 100 employees, he brought an awareness of that concept to each and every employee.

"I was brought in to try to give more of a leadership direction to the mid-level management team," said Michael. "I ended up computerizing the whole operation, and I rewrote the training and evaluations manuals. I dealt with all of the line managers and tried to restructure the way that they dealt with the people under them. And as I did that I was thinking not as an MBA student trained in leadership management, but rather as a bass player.

"We're all in this together," said Michael of the philosophy that he conveyed to the organization. "Anything you do is going to affect me. Anything the person that works under you does is going to affect you. I really tried to get them to understand that the synergies that existed were too complex for them to really understand and to say, 'Here's how this works,' but I wanted them to at least be aware of those synergies. I worked to try to increase awareness of everything they were doing. It was a question of reorienting the way people thought about work and the way they thought about working with each other."

The thoughts that Michael articulated that I found most fascinating were on the subject of risk. It is accepted as a necessary element of the jazz improvisational experience in the quest to discover new ideas.

"I think the biggest thing that business can learn from art in terms of risk is that the whole idea of risk in business is very much shaped from a paradigm in which business was structured around predictability – systems that would constantly work in a very predictable way – the elimination of uncertainty," Michael explained. "The way we define risk is still very much based in the collective experience of business that comes from the last century. These things have radically changed. I don't think anybody would argue that."

Michael then discussed his perspective on the future of Corporate America. "In America, any job that can be done by a computer or menial labor, that's gone. What we're left with – we are the idea factory. We are the people that have in some ways, earned the right to come up with all of the new ideas. If we pull with us into that context the idea that risk means the elimination of uncertainty, we will never come up with any new ideas."

Michael then explained the concept of risk as it applies to jazz, with an underlying message that can provide a blueprint for the innovative 21st century business.

"What's going on in jazz is that we are constantly taking the risk of prototyping new ideas," said Michael. "That's what improvisation means. We're working off of a shared underlying vision, not just pulling music out of thin air. We have a structure. But it's set up in such a way that enables us to constantly take the risk of trying new ideas. And when they work, they change the structure. And that changes the possibilities of what we can come up with. Risk becomes an element that is no longer a choice.

"If we want to be a culture of innovation, which essentially we've set up for ourselves, we have to redefine how we take risks and how we think about risk," he added.

"How do you create a community of thinking in business?" Michael offered as food for thought. "Business has to drive this. I really maintain that business is one of the biggest art forms the world has ever known. Business creates the reality that we live in. How do you get business people to start thinking in terms of the process that many artists have to think about?"

For Michael, the answer to that question is to vividly demonstrate the lessons of the jazz combo for corporate and academic audiences. As a former educator, he understands that in some respects he is facing a menacing task, as teaching adults these lessons is far more difficult than instilling a creative mindset in them from a very young age. He offered an educational remedy for the future.

"Once kids are out of school or once they've gotten to high school even, they're formed," he said. "If you don't get them really young, then you're going to have a difficult time trying to work it in at a later point. The way we're going to redefine risk and understand creativity and how it needs to be a part of every minute of every day of everybody's life, is in primary education."

Dr. Michael White, Educator & Clarinetist

Jazz Clarinetist, Educator
National Endowment of the Arts
National Heritage Fellowship recipient
Presenter: *Teaching Kids Life Lessons Through Jazz* lecture series

"Even if you go into more conventional areas such as business, industry, or politics, the opportunity to teach creativity and teamwork works the same way that it works in jazz. If you learn those concepts early on, you'll be a more flexible and well-rounded person – able to deal with different situations and personalities."

* * *

"What people need to realize is that music can make a tremendous difference in people's lives – even those that are not musicians. It's an alternative to sports to teach you values such as teamwork, individual challenge, and development. It's a way of learning self-respect and respecting others. Those things can be applied to every area of life."

Dr. Michael White is a traditional jazz clarinetist, a music educator, and a music historian. He is a living New Orleans musical link in a chain that connects brass band musicians born in the late 19th century to the vibrant young practitioners of that genre in modern day New Orleans. His ongoing efforts to bridge the generations, to recognize its pioneers, and to continue to practice his craft were recently recognized in 2008 by the National Endowment of the Arts when they awarded Michael the National Heritage Fellowship.

His most recent CD *Blue Crescent* (Basin Street Records 2008) took on the daunting task of conveying through music the disparate emotions of life in New Orleans through the Katrina experience and three years beyond. Michael captures those wide ranging emotions of renewal, loss, joy, fatigue, reflection, longing, and hope brilliantly. The experience of recording the songs and even listening to the finished product was and is deeply emotional for him.

In terms of his calling to music as a career, Michael explains that it was destined since birth, but that it took him a long time to see it. He taught Spanish for years and pursued music as a secondary vocation until he realized that it was truly a viable alternative. "I never really took it [music] seriously because I listened to and believed stereotypes about musicians having a difficult life – late hours and the seedy side of life. It turned out quite different for me in that regard," he said. "I didn't think it was something steady enough. But I never stopped playing, I always practiced, and it just grew from there."

Michael explained that he continued to refine his craft to the point that eventually music became a central focus in his life. "It [music] gradually evolved, and as it evolved it began to push out every other thing in my life little by little, until it became a prominent thing," he said. "Each stage was like a school. It's like I moved in different stages and levels.

"The song 'He Leads Me on This Journey' (from his 2008 CD *Blue Crescent)* related to Katrina – the experience of everybody being at a different stage of recovery and how faith can help us through it," he said. "But it also is about life's journey. I feel very fortunate to have music because it's something that keeps me young and keeps me growing. It's always challenging. That journey is a long journey. I discovered quite a lot writing the songs on this CD that I didn't know about the music and about myself."

Michael now has a greater appreciation for the musical culture of New Orleans that was such an integral part of his formative years. "More than ever I have a renewed sense that New Orleans music and culture are very important and need to be preserved, perpetuated, and spread around the world," said Michael. "We need to recognize and uphold our traditions, because they could be lost just as easily as everything else."

It's Michael's understanding of the New Orleans brass band culture, his awareness of the ongoing evolution of traditional New

Orleans jazz, and his vast musical resume that crosses numerous generations that make his musical background truly unique. That body of work includes time spent with Ernest "Doc" Paulin, a legend of New Orleans brass and dance bands who passed away in 2007 at the age of 100. He mentored dozens if not hundreds of musicians, including Michael.

"I was with 'Doc' Paulin and then with the Fairview (Baptist Church) Band for about four years," said Michael. "I spent a period playing with some of the other traditional groups that played on the streets in the French Quarter. Then I started to have this association with older musicians for many years. I spent a lot of time playing with these guys born before 1910. That was a great experience. Then I moved on to starting my own groups, stretching out and playing with different musicians."

As difficult as it has been for many of the New Orleans musicians to persist in keeping their music careers intact, Michael explains that he really had no other choice. "I don't think I would have survived if it wasn't for music. I don't think I would be in New Orleans right now. Music offers a lot of possibilities in terms of its therapeutic value."

My interest in interviewing Michael did not simply stem from his considerable musical talents. He gives a lecture entitled *Teaching Kids Life Lessons Through Jazz* and has therefore given a great deal of thought to those qualities that children can develop through music that transcend the arts. His familiarity with the New Orleans brass band phenomenon that is as much a neighborhood cultural and generational celebration as it is a musical concept further defines his expertise in the area of music as a developmental tool. He has been a witness to how a culture of music can influence children and change their lives. He shared some of those thoughts.

"What people need to realize is that music can make a tremendous difference in people's lives – even those that are not musicians," he said. "It's an alternative to sports to teach you values such as teamwork, individual challenge, and development. It's a way of learning self-respect and respecting others. Those things can be applied to every area of life.

"In New Orleans we have such an abundance of talent," he added. "We have an environment in which music is part of the street culture in the community and part of commercial life for both musicians and related careers that we desperately need."

Michael explained that forms of expression such as music are catalysts in teaching a student to find their own identity – a way of tapping into your emotions rather than suppressing them. The importance of that gift cannot be overstated. As I've stated previously, it's my belief that the greatest inefficiencies in our world are a result of people avoiding the pursuit of endeavors about which they are passionate and that they are uniquely qualified to achieve because of fear, complacency, or the expectations of others.

If music can be a vehicle to help young people get beyond those limiting behaviors, then teaching students to find their own identity could be the single greatest benefit of music education!

"It's [music] a way of learning to develop individuality in a conformist society, which can be a great thing," he explained. "In New Orleans we have a unique opportunity with music to have people participate either as instrumentalists or as dancers, but both doing the same thing – enhancing creativity and individuality.

"As a teacher, the one thing that concerns me the most is people not discovering themselves," he added. "You never know what's inside of them. You can come along and get a job, a house, and a car and never find out what's inside of you. You might have something great inside of you that you can use and share that gives you a whole other kind of life. It's very important in terms of development."

Once again, Michael reiterated that the concepts learned through music are applicable beyond the world of the professional musician.

"Even if you go into more conventional areas such as business, industry, or politics, the opportunity to teach creativity and teamwork works the same way that it works in jazz," he explained. "If you learn those concepts early on, you'll be a more flexible and well-rounded person – able to deal with different situations and personalities."

Michael then reflected on some of the lessons that he learned through music during his formative years. St. Augustine High School's "Marching 100" is one of the most prestigious and dynamic high school marching bands in New Orleans, a city that is world renowned for its music. Michael reflected on his time as member of that group.

"It challenges you. It gives you the chance to develop and grow as a person, the mind and the character, and to gain skills that you can use in any area. I learned so many things that I used in music and everyday life. I learned discipline, I learned competition, I learned how to win, and I learned how to lose. I learned about sectional pride which involved teamwork. I learned how to listen to different sounds, styles, and instruments. I learned how to lead and how to follow."

Karen Nisenson, Founder/Executive Director & Pianist/Music Therapist/ Music Educator

Founder & Executive Director, Arts for Healing,
Creative Arts Therapy Center non-profit
Pianist, Composer, Music Therapist, Music Educator

"It's [running an organization] like an orchestra or band. As a conductor, you have to know all of the parts, and you have to understand the contributions of each person and understand how it all comes together. No one part is more important than the other. Each part is as important."

* * *

"An organization, like a piece of music, has a form, and it has a structure. Every person who works there, even the client makes up the fabric of the organization. With that attitude, it can go forward in a really great way."

Karen Nisenson is the founder and Director of Arts for Healing, a non-profit organization in New Canaan, Connecticut that uses music and arts therapy to treat special needs patients with developmental disabilities such as Autism, Down Syndrome, and Alzheimer's. Her story is relevant in the context of this book for a number of reasons. First and foremost, the organization is demonstrating tangible results that are currently being documented in clinical research studies. It's a clear demonstration that we are only beginning to understand the power of music and its potential in reaching through to the human mind and spirit – all the more reason to take another look at potential outcomes that could apply to success in business and any number of other areas.

The fact that the community has seen the results and is now beginning to budget funds in the public schools to have access to the services that Karen's group provides only validates that she is reaching a point of critical mass.

"I believe in what I'm doing," said Karen. "I believe that I have something to offer. Nobody else is doing what I'm doing, and I want to see changes in the special needs community. One in 150 babies is being born with developmental disorders, which is very scary. That will be the tipping point that changes children's education. It's going to have to change."

The reaction of the community to the work of Arts for Healing provides evidence supporting what I hope is a trend – a re-thinking of the way music is integrated more seamlessly into the mainstream curriculum rather than being labeled with the dreaded "elective" classification.

Karen's story also illustrates a lesson in conviction. She has faced the challenge of educating the public on the merits of the services that she provides through a period when music and arts therapy was only beginning to be understood. As a single moth-er of five with no support, she had to maintain the faith that if she kept pursuing what she believed in, things would somehow work out.

Never has the need for conviction in your business mission been so critical, with so many people leaving large companies to pursue self-employment as a result of either downsizing or dis-satisfaction. Only a sense of purpose will enable small business leaders to forge ahead in the face of the myriad of obstacles and trials that they will inevitably face.

Karen grew up on 96th and Broadway in Manhattan and lived next door to pianist Leon Fleisher, a gifted pianist, composer, and conductor who would later be honored by the Kennedy Center. She recalled vivid memories of visiting him and seeing those black and white keys as early as the time she was only three years old. She also remembered playing songs like "My Country 'Tis of Thee" and "Fur Elise," and she successfully auditioned for Julliard's preparatory division by the time she was five.

Though her status as a child prodigy might have given an indication of a traditional path of music performance or instruction, it was clear that Karen was keenly aware of the effect of music on emotions, a sensitivity that foreshadowed her eventual career direction. She hinted at that awareness when I asked her how music changed her development as a child and as an adolescent.

"It [music] provided an outlet. It provided a mirror of how I was feeling so that I could understand myself on a deeper level," she said. "It always was there for me. In difficult times, I could always just play. It provided me with comfort, security, stability, expression, and a whole world that was available to me in terms of composition."

At that point, however, Karen was unaware of a field of study related to those emotions. "I was a graduate student at Juilliard, and I was studying composition and piano. I had a teacher that I talked to about the way chords affect feelings," she said. "I never knew anything about the field of music therapy."

Karen's instructor referred her to a composer friend by the name of Paul Nordoff. She told Karen, "He speaks like you. He talks about the same things in his compositions. He's doing this thing in Europe called music therapy with this special education teacher, Clyde Robbins."

Karen's instructor then showed her a black and white film developed by these early pioneers of music therapy. "I looked at this film and saw this man sitting at the piano improvising music that completely mirrored the personalities of these kids who had autism," Karen said. "When the child in the film opened her eyes wide and realized that someone was speaking to her on a deep level through the music, that struck me. There was a feeling of 'I can do that.'"

After receiving her Masters at Juilliard in piano performance, she went on to NYU and earned a Masters degree in music therapy.

"There was nothing available in New Canaan, Connecticut in terms of arts therapy," Karen said. "What they had in the school system in terms of music therapy was so limited. It didn't go nearly to the depths that I was getting into with the kids. I was affiliated with the Nordoff-Robbins Center for Music Therapy at the time.

"I had to stay here full-time because of a lot of personal transition," she added. "I've been a single mother of five kids for many, many years. I didn't want to get a job somewhere because it would be so confining for me, and I wouldn't be able to do my particular thing, which is music and arts therapy combined. So I decided to start a center. I did it non-profit so that we could get the money to start it right away."

Arts for Healing is currently funded through a combination of grants, donations, and fees from clients. Karen credits Joseph Dionne, a Former CEO of McGraw-Hill, for support in the early stages of the organization that was critical in getting things off the ground. "He had two sons who had significant developmental issues," she said. "He understood the world of special needs, and he was a philanthropist. He helped start the organization financially."

I believe that the general public has only a vague conception of how music and the arts are used in a therapeutic manner, and I can't say that I had a clear understanding prior to meeting Karen. She told a story that I found enlightening in terms of understanding the process of how the magic of music therapy works.

"When a child comes in who has autism, who can't speak, who is non-verbal for example, you can make music out of anything they do," she explained. "Let's say they take a drumstick and beat on the drum as I improvise something on the piano. All of a sudden they are part of something. They feel that they are in a conversation. These improvisations then get developed into back and forth talking musically.

"Ultimately, they feel part of a communication that they're not used to," she added. "That translates within six months into vocalization. I have a microphone, they start singing, they start making sounds, and the relationship develops. These kinds of kids have not developed relationships because of their disabilities.

"When you can form a relationship through music and improvisation, you create a safe and nurturing environment where the kids can re-experience the stages of development that they missed," she explained. "In speaking and language development, babbling is something that babies have to do before they can say a word, but kids with autism or severe developmental disabilities don't do that."

Karen explained that during her study of music therapy, the curriculum included lots of psychology, science, and special education courses. Her work in creative arts therapy became a synthesis of psychoanalytic theory, music, and art.

It's clear that Karen's success is based in part due to the fact that she understands individuality. Throughout her career she has taken pride in ensuring that music students and arts therapy patients receive an approach tailored to their needs.

"I teach kids with learning disabilities and I teach kids piano who are on the autism spectrum," she noted. "I've taught at NYU for 25 years, so I've taught docile students and very advanced players. I think what you have to do is understand who the person is, number one. You understand the age of the person, the level of the person, what are they capable of in terms of cognitive learning, how they learn, and their learning style.

"How do you draw the line between challenging and being able to accomplish something?" she said of that fine line that music instructors must walk to be successful. "That's really important. If it's too hard, it only leads to frustration. If you can recognize the strengths of the student and work with that and make them feel each time that they've accomplished something, that's really the most important thing, no matter what level."

She then recollected one of her early instructors at Julliard who possessed many of those qualities, Mr. Jones. "He had all of these [qualities]. I was only five or six. He made it seem fun and easy. This man made me feel so comfortable. There was no judgment."

Because Karen studied at such a high level of excellence and expectation with some of the most esteemed mentors in music, she inspires that spirit in her organization and in her employees.

"I think a very important component that I bring to the work is having gone to a conservatory like Julliard, I was exposed to a very high level aesthetic," she said. "I think that I bring that into the work with every child. I bring a level to each child of the best that they can be. I bring that level of expertise into the organization, so that anyone who comes to work there has to be on that kind of level as well. And I think that's why it's working in the community."

Karen then used a music analogy to describe the success of her organization and her approach to any creative endeavor.

"It's like an orchestra or band," she explained. "As a conductor, you have to know all of the parts, you have to understand the contributions of each person, and understand how it all comes together. It's an interwoven whole. Like a conductor, I try to understand all the different parts and make it come together. No one part is more important than the other. Each part is as important.

"An organization, like a piece of music, has a form, and it has a structure," she added. "I try to look at that. I am just part of the whole. I'm not removed in any way. Every person who works there, even the client, makes up the fabric of the organization. With that attitude, it can go forward in a really great way."

She believes that too many people today get hung up on their little parts. "Every creative project is like a soup," she explained. "You have to let go of your ingredients for the sake of the soup. If you can't, you shouldn't be in the project. If you have to hold on to your ingredient and make a big deal that it's yours, then it won't work. That's my philosophy of any creative project that I'm part of as well as the organization."

Perhaps Arts for Healing is a spark that can ignite a flame by demonstrating the success of creative arts therapy that can be replicated elsewhere.

"It's grown a lot," Karen said with pride. "We have programs in the schools. Kids that were coming to us privately, they saw a difference in how they listened to the teachers and how they related in the classroom. Then parents started saying, 'Why can't my children get music therapy in school?'

"They have really acknowledged that music helped tremendously," she added. "All of the positives of music that applied to me also apply to kids with special needs, and improvements in language development, socialization, fine and gross motor skills – everything gets better through music and the art. We've helped a lot of kids along the way.

"We started that about three years ago. They were seeing a real difference in the kids, so they budgeted money for the music therapy. Now the school system recognizes that this really has to be incorporated into the system."

Karen acknowledged that she still has her own form of music therapy so to speak, composing music. She articulated her approach to finding that space where creative ideas emerge.

"It's really letting go of the self and getting into a place of openness," she confided. "Put yourself in the idea. It's my favorite place to be, and it's one that gives me my greatest joy – being able to be in 'that place.' It's timeless, it's a very spiritual place, and it's a discovery place. It's one that you don't control. You let it happen. If you don't let go and your mind controls it, it won't work. Always aware of the goals and the direction it's taking, but really letting it happen."

Neil Moore, Founder/Executive Director & Pianist

Founder & Executive Director, *Simply Music*
Pianist

"We don't spend enough time really looking at what is the psychological impact on a child when they are able to connect to this natural dimension [music] of being human. I assert that absolutely every single human being is profoundly musical."

* * *

"I'm of the view that when you create populations of people who are profoundly musical and give them an education system that does not let them access their musicality, we don't have even the capacity to begin quantifying the cost of that on a global level – can't even begin to quantify it."

Neil is the founder and Executive Director of *Simply Music*. The company is a platform for sharing Neil's unique methodology for piano instruction that accelerates the student's ability to play and allows people without a formal music education to pass along those lessons.

Often during these interviews I've allowed the subjects to digress from the strict subject matter of the correlation between music and business, if their insights were valuable in understanding the power of music and music education in a broader context. Often their digressions also gave me a glimpse into their own personal journey in life. I gave Neil carte blanche in that regard, because his life experiences have given him so many lessons and opportunities to explore the impact of music, and his thoughts were fascinating and inspiring.

Neil's pathway into music as a career could be characterized as serendipitous, if not accidental.

Neil's parents were both music lovers, and as the youngest of five children he was expected to take piano lessons starting at age seven, just as all of his elder siblings had done. His parents recalled that Neil had a strong connection to music even before he was old enough to play. "I would roll into whatever room music was being played and just lie there," he shared from his parents' recollection. "There was some connection and mesmerization that I had with music long before I even had consciousness of myself."

Neil began to develop a unique conceptualization of music from an early age. "I hear music and I see two and three dimensional shapes," he explained. "I would draw mental pictures, and I would organize those pictures sequentially. I would draw these visual maps of the pieces I was hearing. That was a more important foundation for me than I'd ever realized."

When he began piano at the age of seven, his teacher would play, and, unbeknownst to his teacher, Neil visualized shapes. Even though he was supposed to be learning how to read music notation, that's not what occurred. When he would hear the music and visualize those shapes, he could just position his hands on the keyboard. That was the basis of how he learned to play.

"The next week when I was having my lesson where I was supposed to be music reading, I would just sit there and stare at the page blankly," he said. "I was thinking that if I look at the page, I'm fooling my teacher, and he'll think that I'm reading. I made no connection to the page at all. I didn't learn to read music until I was in my 30s."

It is ironic that Neil's simplified method for conceptualizing and playing music, which would later provide a foundation for his life's work, was a source of shame for many years.

"By the time I was 12, I was playing a pretty reasonable repertoire," said Neil. "I always felt like I was cheating. I wasn't doing the 'real' thing. So I kept it hidden from people. I didn't even share with people in the outside world much that I played at all, because I was terrified that someone would put some music in front of me and ask me to play and I would be 'found out.' I had this fraudulent relationship with it. As much as music became this place where I would just immerse myself, it was never done in a public environment."

It's truly amazing that Neil's organization has impacted music learning on a global basis when you consider the fact that he grew up in a geographic location where access to music was somewhat limited.

"The longing to pursue music was always with me," he said. "Growing up in Australia where even though it's a contemporary society, a much smaller population doesn't afford the same choices and opportunities. For example, the only jazz that was played was one hour on Friday night on a program called *Music to Midnight.* It ran from 11 o'clock to midnight on our government radio station."

Neil was a fan of swing music from a very early age. He recalled having to order imported vinyl records from a catalog and then having to wait three months for them to arrive. Music was considered to be a great thing and a valuable thing, but not something you could do as a profession.

Neil came from a family of non-academics – self-employed, business savvy people. His parents were very involved in the community, and there was always an expectation that Neil would follow a similar path. As such, he became quite successful in the restaurant business and in middle management in the wine industry retail sector. "The view for me was 'If I can get into business, do really well, and make enough money, then I can retire out of that and just do whatever I want to in music,'" said Neil of his master plan.

Everything was proceeding essentially according to his plan. He was running successful businesses and building a traditional stable financial base. And then came a turn of events that could only be seen as good fortune in retrospect. Neil took over a business that had all of its assets tied up in the stock market, and it was "hemorrhaging cash" at one point according to Neil. That error in judgment translated into a complete financial wipeout for him. He lost everything. He recalled having to sell jewelry to be able to buy food for his family.

In that period of desperation came the turning point for Neil and his passion for music.

"There was a particular day where I remembered that our cars were repossessed," he revealed. "I just had this moment of realizing 'They're taking away everything physical, but they're taking nothing of me that matters. Who I am is whole and intact.' It was just one of those moments. I just sort of made a pact that I would never pursue money as a means of then pursuing my love. I would pursue what I always thought I was called to do. I would pursue that and trust that if I do what I'm meant to do, I'll be taken care of along the way.

"I remember that day. I remember the time of day. I remember the weather and where I was standing. It was an instant in my life. Even then I didn't know what [my future] was going to look like. At that point in time I'm not an accomplished player, I can't read music, and I don't understand music theory. I've never taught a person music in my life. All I know is that there's nothing more that I love, nothing more that I feel connected to than music."

Neil later started a program of music studies at the most prestigious music education institution in Australia, the Victorian College of the Arts. The university began to make available "Saturday school," a program open to anyone on weekends without any entrance requirements. He took jazz studies and theory courses and absolutely loved it. He soon was able to bring the traditionally accepted language of music to that which he could do but of which he had no formal understanding.

He also came across another gentleman who offered a music reading program, and Neil attended his weekend workshop. Neil's perspective provided valuable input during the sessions, and the gentleman was impressed enough that he asked Neil to join his organization as an instructor. Neil began to teach both students and instructors in this reading-based methodology.

Neil's wife had a great experience several years earlier as an exchange student in the U.S., and Neil had a desire to get to what he called the epicenter of the jazz and R&B music that he loved. So they relocated to California to bring that reading-based music program to the U.S. While Neil had now aligned his choice of vocation with his life's joy, there remained a disharmony so to speak between the methodologies he was teaching and those that he himself employed when learning music as a child.

"My feeling always was that there was a fundamental disconnect," Neil explained. "Even though I was teaching this reading-based approach, it wasn't the affinity of my natural approach to music. I got a call from a government agency one day and they asked if I would take on teaching this eight-year old blind boy. I said, 'This will be fun. Absolutely, I'd love to do that.' For me it was, 'How am I going to do this?' Well heck, I didn't need to read music. I wonder if I could do with him what I did for myself."

Until that point, Neil never even considered the possibility of consciously exploring the way that music occurred to him as a child. "I sat down and said, 'Let me just take some of these pieces that I'm teaching and examine how would I have learned these pieces as a kid without any music reading,' and I just started to explain these in terms of shapes and patterns and putting language to it," said Neil. "I was turning around with this eight-year old boy during the week and giving him a lesson, and it was amazing how quickly he was learning to play. And I thought, 'Oh well, being without sight, he's got a really developed set of ears, and that's what's guiding his way.'

"About three months down the track this kid had a repertoire of 12 to 15 contemporary blues songs and classical pieces – stuff that I just assembled using the shape-based approach," said Neil. "I said to his dad one day, 'Are you happy with his progress?' He said, 'Not only are we happy with it, but he's turned around and he's teaching his four-year old sister how to play this way. And she's blind, too.'

"This was another moment where I knew my life would never be the same," he added. "I thought, 'Wow, what would happen if I taught this to all young children?' I started developing the concepts and sharing them with other young children. What shocked me was these kids started to play not only more sophisticated music more quickly, but the connection to the music was so much more natural."

From that moment, Neil expanded his shape-based approach to music education, setting up lesson plans, sharing information with instructors, and test-marketing his approach with others who could communicate their findings when applying his concepts. "I started sharing this with some of the teachers that I knew and said, 'Try this and see if you can do this yourself,'" Neil said. "They came back saying, 'Wow, this is really something.'"

Simply Music was founded to provide a platform for formalizing his methods and sharing them in an organized manner.

"It was very obvious that in the learning of this, people were also inheriting the ability to teach others," said Neil of the realization of the far-reaching potential his methods had. "We could really impact the whole culture of music education here if I could develop it in not only a way that it gave a new level of access to students, but it also could be taught by people who were not formally trained musicians – not experienced teachers. I knew that it went against the grain, but I just didn't care. For the first time ever I felt that my point of view had application.

"These people are playing great music, and they're loving it," said Neil with enthusiasm. "The vast majority of people don't want to elevate up to adult concert level performance. What people want to have and what people need is to have music as a companion in their lives."

Neil began to share his methodologies with young and old, those with developmental disabilities, and with troubled youth in inner city schools – those kids who, in their teachers' words, could succeed at absolutely nothing. And Neil had success in all of those challenging situations.

Neil has found that his approach to music has had far-reaching application beyond music. "I organize things," Neil explained. "I found that there's a very direct correlation between organization and creativity. In the restaurant industry that I was involved in, the chef had a reputation of being hot-tempered. A lot of that had to do with the fact that no one had taught [the restaurant workers] basic principles of organization. My principles of developing organization had come about directly as a result of the way that I organized shapes and patterns in music.

"I always saw a direct correlation," he added. "I would watch the way people would physically work, and the way that I saw that was the way that I would hear music. I would see repetition of physical gestures, and I would see more efficient ways of organizing those gestures. I would see people do things one after the other, and I would say, 'You know what – if you would organize them in a different way, you'd get a far better result. You could get to the end result more quickly.' Even though I was talking about that in what might have been an administrative position, it was always very clear to me that it was exactly the way music occurred to me. It had come from my relationship with music."

Neil now sees his mission in life clearly – giving massive populations of people access to musicianship – not with the goal and intention of these people elevating to adult concert-level performance, but not doing anything to get in the way of that, either. "That's wonderful and important," said Neil. "It's just not what the vast majority wants and needs."

Neil's sentiments support my view that justifying music education on the basis that it improves math or science scores is a flawed approach because it implies that music is a lesser priority and discounts other more important benefits. His thoughts and those of the music enthusiasts with whom he has discussed these ideas were very revealing.

Neil stated, "The data that's emerging over the past 15 years, while I find that data interesting, I'm actually not a strong proponent of the data (referring to the research that illustrates that music improves I.Q. scores and the understanding of spatial relationships). Neil then articulated some of the talking points from his own focus group research. "The first question I ask is, 'How many people really know your I.Q.?'" he explained. "It's amazing how few people really know their I.Q. The second question I ask is, 'If any one of you could improve your I.Q. a few percentage points, how do you really believe it would make a difference to the actual experience and quality of your life?' And no one actually knows.

"So while we have that data, I don't think that's what people care about," Neil concluded. "When I get in rooms of people, and I have lots of opportunity to do this, I say, 'Tell me what it really means to you that you have the ability to play music.' And it is eye-opening when people who've been able to keep music as a companion are asked, 'What are the five most important things in life – period?' Even though the order is different, people usually say:

- ❏ Their spiritual relationship
- ❏ Their relationship with their spouse and children
- ❏ Their physical well-being
- ❏ Their financial well-being
- ❏ Music

"It might be in a different order for different people, but typically people who've kept music late into their lives rank it as being one of the five most important things in their life," he said.

"When we talk about what it is that they love [about music], they say:

- ❏ This is how I pray
- ❏ This is how I heal myself
- ❏ I use this as a means of socialization
- ❏ This is how I contribute to other people
- ❏ This is my means of worship
- ❏ This is my means of entertaining others
- ❏ I love the challenge of it, the puzzle of it
- ❏ I find that it's my place of solitude, my place of rest
- ❏ This is where I experience the real essence of being human

"My experience when working with younger children is that the importance of music is not so much math scores and improving their I.Q. We don't spend enough time really looking at what is the psychological impact on a child when they are able to connect to this natural dimension of being human," Neil asserted. "I assert that absolutely every single human being is profoundly musical.

"When you and I are walking down the street engaged in a dialogue, we're oblivious to the fact that we're walking with perfectly natural, even, smooth rhythm," he said. "Whether you're hammering a nail, sawing wood, or brushing your teeth, everything is underscored by this profound sense of musicality. I'm of the view that when you create populations of people who are profoundly musical and give them an education system that does not let them access their musicality, we don't have even the capacity to begin quantifying the cost of that on a global level. Can't even begin to quantify it," he repeated emphatically.

"If we can open the door to that and give people access to their musicality, it impacts their self-esteem, it impacts their view of who they are in the world, and it impacts their ability to be creative," Neil said of the universal benefits of music. "And where creativity is so profound is that creativity is the solution for managing our problems. We're teaching kids how to manage problems in school, but the reality of the situation is that we have no idea what the world is going to look like in five years. That is the problem. How do you teach adaptability? You cannot teach adaptability if you take out of the education system access to creativity. You can't do it."

Willie Jolley, Professional Speaker & Vocalist/Trumpet Player
Professional Speaker
Vocalist and trumpet player
5-time Washington Area Music Association
(WAMMIE) Award Winner

"In music, the best improvisation was often rehearsed scales or fundamentals that you took somewhere else. In business, you've got a business plan, you've thought it through, but something changes. You can then take that business plan and alter it or augment it or diminish it, and it has an impact on your business."

* * *

"Learning music is like taming a tiger. You've got to find new ways and new things and new gifts that you have within you. When you can reach a new way of thinking, it impacts you in many ways. When they start taking music out of the schools it's a major, major mistake."

When people think of music and speaking, Willie Jolley is one of the top people who come to mind. His clients, companies such as Verizon Communications, Ford Motor Company, and Wal-Mart Corporation, agree. Willie has also shared the stage with world renowned singer Gladys Knight and has been recognized in the "best jazz singer" and "best entertainer" categories by the Washington Area Music Association.

When Willie was a youth, he would only do background vocals. He refused to stand out in front because he lacked confidence in his abilities. During one performance where he was playing the trumpet in a band, his parents asked him, "Why aren't you singing with that band?" Willie replied, "I don't know."

So Willie asked the band if he could sing, and they said, "Okay."

"One guy who I thought was my friend started laughing," said Willie. "When he laughed, everybody snickered or giggled, and I was embarrassed. I said, 'I'll never do that again.' And that had a major impact," Willie said emphatically. "I didn't sing for years in anything but the background."

Those doubts were washed away with one shining experience that he recalled vividly in which music empowered him with unwavering confidence.

"One night I was at a club, and the singer didn't show up. They said, 'We need somebody to sing.' I said, 'I can't sing.' They said, 'You either sing or you're fired.' I started singing because I had to," said Willie. "I closed my eyes and started singing as loud and as strong as I could. People stopped dancing and started looking, and they started clapping. And I realized that my friend had lied to me."

Willie's friend planted the seed of doubt, and Willie watered and fertilized it over the years. "I grew it in my mind that I couldn't sing," he admitted. "If I had not listened to his negative comments, I would have been singing early on. Once I started singing that night, people started asking if I could sing at their wedding, their graduation, their reception."

Once Willie became confident as a lead vocalist, he pursued singing and music as a career.

"By the time I was in college, I was paying my way through college by singing jingles and singing studio sessions," he said.

"Every way you could make a living singing, I was doing it: singing at theaters, singing at funerals, weddings. I became a professional singer after graduate school and did that for about seven years.

"My career shifted because the industry changed," he reflected. "They were moving more toward disco and karaoke. I was very frustrated because I couldn't actively pursue what I wanted to do. My last job at the night club, they fired the band because the karaoke machine was cheaper."

It was a tremendous blow for someone who had envisioned himself as part of a musical ensemble since he and his brother had drawn pictures of themselves playing the Beatles' instruments in the first grade. Willie had honed his considerable musical talents through years of work and had developed a versatility that allowed him to work in a wide range of musical situations. His influences included Al Jarreau, Bobby McFerrin, Stevie Wonder, Frank Sinatra (for his phrasing), and Ella Fitzgerald (for her ability to scat). All of those aspirations and hard work had seemingly been for naught.

But then, a twist of fate changed Willie's career path.

"Somebody knew of my musical background and the fact that I had a graduate degree in counseling," said Jolley. "They said, 'We need you to be part of a new program. We're using music, arts, and drama as a part of a drug prevention vehicle. We'd like you to coordinate this because of your background.'"

It was at that point that Willie realized that he could connect with an audience in a more profound way by adding music to the presentation.

"As part of my job I had to give little presentations, and I learned that I could speak," he said. "I mixed my music with the speaking, and it took off. Music reached people in different ways.

Even people who you can't reach verbally, sometimes you can reach with music. So it's a very powerful tool."

Whether speaking to corporate executives or troubled youths, Willie has used music to inspire, transform, and empower his audiences. But he also found music to be an excellent tool in terms of the way it trained him to cultivate his unique gifts and realize his potential.

"Music will create a thinking apparatus that would never come to light otherwise – the things that I had to think about with music and how I had to practice and prepare myself. Learning music is like taming a tiger," he explained. "You've got to find new ways and new things and new gifts that you have within you. When you can reach a new way of thinking, it impacts you in many ways. When they start taking music out of the schools it's a major, major mistake."

Willie is appreciative of the improvisational nature of music, lessons that he has been able to draw upon in his speaking business that allow him to maintain an even keel when things don't go quite as planned.

"I learned how to be improvisational when I was on stage. Sometimes I didn't know the words, or we wanted to take the band somewhere else – these arrangements that we created [by improvising] on stage were just wonderful. The same is true for business. Sometimes things don't go as planned. You've got to improvise. You've got to think on your feet and come up with some new strategies – try this, let's go here.

"In music, the best improvisation was often rehearsed scales or fundamentals that you took somewhere else. In business, you've got a business plan. You've thought it through, but something changes. You can then take that business plan and alter it or augment it or diminish it, and it has an impact on your business."

Willie also articulated the parallels between a musician connecting with an audience and a business professional connecting with a potential customer.

"In business, you can change someone's thinking by changing the tone, the volume, and the intensity [of the conversation]. All of those things are part of the musical experience."

As we have discussed previously, you should think of creativity as a muscle – the more you use it (your creative "muscle") the stronger it gets. And once that muscle is developed and toned, it can apply to any endeavor, musical or otherwise. Willie echoed those sentiments from his own experience.

"I'm always hearing a beat in my head, some sort of a rhythm. That's constant with me. I'm tapping my foot and my wife's asking, 'What are you hearing.' I'm always thinking about how I can color that beat. The same is true for creativity," he explained. "How do I take that which is the basis and then build on it? And how do I take my business and build on it, and see things that are not there yet, but try new things?"

Dara Turetsky, Founding Director & Pianist

Founding Director, Colour Me Music
Music Educator, Pianist/Songwriter of
the band Acoustik Solution
(Pictured with daughter Olivia)

"When creativity is put into business, it flourishes. When creativity is removed, people are bored, they're stifled, and they hate their jobs. Music induces creativity. If you're not creative, you can't think of new ideas to solve problems."

* * *

"Music is a process. All adults should take music lessons because they'll understand the processes. Creativity is structured. Even when you're creating, you still need a starting point and an end point."

Dara Turetsky is the Director and founder of Colour Me Music, a music education company founded in Long Island, New York and later relocated to Coral Springs, Florida. All music instruction is designed to develop effective and efficient learners, hence the tagline: "Music Programs for Developing Minds." Dara feels strongly that the skills that she teaches her students help prepare them for excellence in all of their endeavors. She explicitly promotes the power of music to help children become effective and efficient learners as a benefit of her teaching programs.

Dara recalled listening to the music of Elton John and learning the melodies on the family's organ as young as the age of four or five years. She also achieved proficiency with the flute, violin, and saxophone at various stages of her musical upbringing. It was a trip to Europe with her family that ignited her passion to pursue music as a serious endeavor.

"I used to travel to Europe with my family. My dad was pretty cosmopolitan, and he took us to an after-hours jazz club in Paris," she recalled with great clarity. "I was 18 years old. I saw this jazz quartet, and I remember thinking when I go back to college I'm going to start a band."

That experience was compelling enough to provoke her to leave college in upstate New York and to transfer to NYU. After a brief stint working for an education company where she trained other teachers, she decided to go out on her own.

Dara claims that she was a natural teacher, and she recalled a ninth grade history teacher – Mr. Mendel – who saw potential in her and set very high expectations. "School came easy to me," Dara said. "He challenged me. He didn't let me 'float.' We did oral reports. Everyone got to pick theirs, and mine was assigned. It was the hardest topic with the least amount of information."

She also has fond memories of another teaching mentor, Nick Ambrosino, who gave her the seal of approval with a simple note that launched her teaching career. "He taught me everything I know about teaching, and then we got to a point where I started creating my own curriculum," she recalled. "He wrote me a letter that said, 'Ah, the student has become the teacher.'"

Music has been a constant in Dara's life. "Music was my salvation as a kid. When you create something it's that feeling of magic you get in your gut. Ah, it's just a spark," she said with emotion. "I always sang, and I was always in the school musicals. Later I was in the choir, and we traveled. I was always involved in music and always did it for fun. But the bug really hit me in college – like this is what I want to do."

But again, it is Dara's emphasis on the developmental skills that are learned in music but applicable universally that I find interesting and particularly relevant in the context of my research. She outlined those skills as follows with a brief illustration of each:

❑ Problem solving
"I had a student who always stopped from line 1 to line 2 [while playing a musical piece]. We identified and addressed all of the potential reasons – looking at his hands and not the music, using a fingering that's not logical, and playing the piece too fast."

❑ Breaking down challenges into doable segments
"You can break down the music segment into measures or into the musical side (notes, rhythms, pitches, harmonies, and melodies) and the technical side (fingering, pedaling, and articulation). You can't think of all of them at once. You need to break it down and determine 'Which one am I going to work on?'

"The overall task is daunting. Breaking down that one larger task made it much more doable and less scary. Practicing is a learned skill. If you don't know how to break down a challenge into doable sections, you can't solve a problem, be it music or math or science."

❑ Creativity
"Music induces creativity. If you're not creative, you can't think of new ideas to solve problems. Einstein said it best, 'Imagination is more important than knowledge.' It's important to know stuff, but it's important to know what to do with it."

❑ Listening
"I consider music a language. If you were teaching a child Mandarin Chinese, you couldn't put Mandarin characters in

front of them and expect them to be successful. Yet traditional teachers will slap a book in front of a five year-old who's not yet even reading their language and ask them to play.

"I teach as young as 2 ½ year-olds. I'll play and ask them 'Do these sound the same or do they sound different? Are these sounds going up or are they going down? Are they long or are they short? And are these connected or are they bouncy?'

"When they learn these different sounds, it's very language-based. Then you put it [a musical piece] in a very general term in front of them and say 'This is what going up looks like. This is what a long note looks like.' They have a basis for what you are talking about, and they're hearing the different sounds."

Dara explained that great listening skills are really what distinguish great musicians as well. "Good musicians are expressive because they're hearing it. They're hearing what the music is asking of them," she said. "If someone is just plunking out notes, you might as well do it on a computer keyboard, because it's the same as typing."

Dara was adamant regarding the importance of tailoring her approach to each student rather than using a generic cookie-cutter approach. "I've had some children with motor coordination issues, and they're looking for a physical experience," she explained. "Some parents just want a diversion for the kids. I teach a girl whose mother plays in an orchestra. She wants her daughter to have a musical experience. The daughter is only three, but let me tell you this kid is great. I teach to the student what the student needs at that moment."

Dara also noted that learning is a two-way street. She recalled a challenging student who was difficult personality-wise, yet talented. "It took me a long time to earn his respect," she noted. "I taught him from the age of eight through his senior year of high school. I thanked him and told him, 'You've made me have to really stretch and think and find a way to teach you specifically.' He was so musical. I taught him piano and he also studied cello and electric guitar. It turns out he actually went to college for music.

"Each kid has something really spectacular to offer me," she added. "You see them go from 'I can't do this' to 'I can do anything.' My students played at my wedding. When I walked down the aisle, I had two violins and a piano."

Dara echoed the sentiments of author John Kao regarding the growing frustration of employees in corporate environments when they are not given an opportunity to innovate and grow. "When creativity is put into business, it flourishes. When creativity is removed, people are bored, they're stifled, and they hate their jobs."

Her brief experience in the corporate world only served to reinforce those frustrations. "I wasn't given any starting points or ending points. I was told 'Here's your seat, here's your task, do it, do 20 others, but I'm not going to tell you what's expected of you. I'm not going to tell you how to do it. Knock yourself out. Do it every day, and don't be late.' It was very frustrating."

While Dara's thoughts confirm the growing collective opinion regarding the critical need for "whole-brained" thinkers in the workplace – those who can balance logical and creative thinking – she makes it a point to drive that concept into her music students too.

"Applying business to music on the flipside, think about all of the great musicians coming out of college," she said. "There are only so many open seats in the orchestra. The guys from the Trans-Siberian Orchestra for example – they created a niche for themselves. They're master musicians, and they're good at business. To balance the two is important. I always lecture my students, 'I don't care what you major in. Make sure you take business classes.'"

So while Dara fine tunes her own creative engine by developing innovative ways to approach each new student, she also writes and records music with her husband Ed, whom she met in a rock band in the 80s. Together they form the duo Acoustik Solution, and their diverse musical interests are reflected in their compositions. As to her inspiration for creativity, let's just say that Ed takes a back seat.

"My dog Charlie is my muse," she claimed. "My classical pieces – each one tells a story. My first one was 'The Many Moods of Charlie.' It goes through four different sections and each one is a different mood. I like to take real life situations and turn them into music."

Dara finds that her process-oriented approach to music has served her well in business, now that she manages a team of music educators. "Music is a process," she said. "All adults should take music lessons because they'll understand the processes. Creativity is structured. Even when you're creating, you still need a starting point and an end point.

"Music is teamwork," she added. "It's process-oriented. It's knowing when to move and knowing when to wait. It's like painting with water colors. You can't overlay another color until the first layer dries. I was working on a Beethoven sonata and getting frustrated. I sat there and said 'You know what, the paint's got to dry.' I had to let once section gel in my head in order to absorb it. Then I was ready for the next step."

Mike Rayburn, Corporate Keynote Performing Guitarist
"The World's Funniest Guitar Virtuoso,"
Classically trained, comically derailed
Carnegie Hall & Corporate Keynote Performer

"Business can be an art. When you approach it from an artistic standpoint, a creative standpoint, a possibilities standpoint, you come up with new things. You look at something different…"

* * *

"I ask the question 'What if?' all of the time."

Mike Rayburn is a talented but unconventional performer. He more than lives up to his tagline as "World's Funniest Guitar Virtuoso." Though his career began as a traditional musician, he considers himself, "Classically trained and comically derailed." A brief look at a few elements of his repertoire explain his madness, as Mike is known for combining musical artists and styles in ways God never intended. "Bob Marley sings Garth Brooks," "Led Zeppelin sings Dr. Seuss," "Dan Fogelberg sings AC/DC," and "Bruce Springsteen sings Green Acres," illustrate my point.

Mike has been featured in *USA Today, Newsweek, Billboard, American Entertainment,* and *Campus Activities Today* magazines. He has performed more than 4,000 shows worldwide, including eight Carnegie Hall appearances.

After a torrid schedule of playing the college circuit, where he played over 1,800 shows in 16 years and was voted college entertainer of the year (2001), Mike turned his focus on the corporate market, playing keynotes and musical asides for the convention and business crowd. Where the term "think outside the box" is often a cliché in the business world, Mike's performance style is a vivid illustration that true creativity comes from having a unique perspective on the world around you.

"My message is a pretty universal one," said Mike. "People always say I want to think outside the box, but no one tells them how to do that. I teach them three tools that I've used throughout the years to look at things differently. It's a light message, but they want a message. What they are looking for is something entertainment-based, but with a message.

"I ask the question 'What if?' all of the time," he added, giving further insight into the core attribute that defines his presentation style. A drive in the car while he was listening to the radio and his children were reading books in the back seat led to the "Led Zeppelin sings Dr. Zeuss" idea, one of his real crowd pleasers. "Someone requested 'Dueling Banjos' and I asked 'What if the banjo player is from Bagdad?'" he said. That inquiry led to "Dueling Banj-arabia," an eclectic mix of eastern and western guitar styles.

Mike's earliest memory of music was singing along to his parents' vinyl albums that he would spin on the old console stereo, most notably Mitch Miller's "When the Red, Red Robin Comes Bob, Bob, Bobbin' Along." While he acknowledges that those who simply listen to music rather than play it can be moved by music and experience its "wow factor," he always felt as though music struck a deeper chord (every pun intended when speaking to Mike) in him. He started playing the old family upright piano at the age of about five or six, and said of that experience, "I always got it. It always made sense to me."

Mike received a guitar for his eighth birthday, and that just set him on the course. "I just loved it," he revealed. "I went in the basement and played. It was my escape.

Specifically, the moment that I knew that I was going to do it for a living was in eighth grade when I performed in a folk concert at the high school. It was very counterintuitive, because I'm from a totally athletic sports family. I did three songs – "Cats in the Cradle," "Dream Weaver," and a John Denver song that no one will remember called "I'm Sorry." I got all of my nervousness for the rest of my life out of the way just before I went on, honestly. I don't think I looked at the audience very much."

Despite a slight case of stage fright, Mike was smitten with the entertainment business.

"I was nervous, but at the same time it just clicked," he said fondly. "I knew this was it. It just hit me on this deeper inner level that it still hits me on today. I didn't know how it was going to materialize, but I knew it then."

Mike studied classical guitar in college and continued to perform as a means of funding his education. It was a series of circumstances that led him to introduce a comedic twist into his performance, one that gives him a niche in the market.

"I had experimented with a whole number of genres of music," said Mike. "I played jazz, I played in rock bands, and I played a solo acoustic thing. The first inkling of where this would go was at some point in high school during a folk concert for the school assembly. I did two funny songs, and they laughed. I loved that.

"Later, I heard a guy named Mike Cross play during my freshman year of college," he recollected. "He's hilarious. After experimenting with all this different music, that was the first time I stood up at the end of a show and said to myself, 'That's what I'm going to do.' After that I started playing bars, and I'm just playing songs, but people would have weird requests. Here I am playing acoustic stuff, and somebody yells out 'Michael Jackson.' I would make a joke about it, or I'd make a parody of it. People started digging that. It was really playing in bars for drunk people."

Mike Rayburn is a walking demonstration of the effect that music can have on creative thought. Not only is his performance style unique, but he also has been able to reinvent himself during transitions from honky-tonk bars to the college circuit to the corporate keynote business. In the process, he has achieved the longevity that only a small percentage of musicians have enjoyed. He is now at the top of his game, enjoying the most successful period of his career, one that has led him to Carnegie Hall performances.

"Music and arts education improve everything," he said. "When you start participating in music, you start opening up the right brain. It gets you into 'possibility thinking.' Music opens up the possibilities.

"Business can be an art," he explained. "When you approach it from an artistic standpoint, a creative standpoint, a possibilities standpoint, you come up with new things. You look at something different.

"I'm speaking to you from an iPhone right now. This thing's just brilliant, and it's because it's different. Somebody looked at the whole thing differently. It [music] helps you look at business as a means of expression, with the point being that it will still translate to a bottom line."

The focus of this book has been to connect the dots between music and business as separate but related pursuits. There are clearly opportunities to directly use music in work environments or in work-related activities as a means to inspire, enhance cohesiveness, and to convey messages in a more constructive manner. Several of our subjects gave such examples, and Mike relayed a story that illustrates why music can be such a prolific tool in those efforts.

"The combination of the emotive value of music, the ability of it to just reach in and grab your heart, and at the same time sharing a message that's congruent with that can hit somebody right when they need it," Mike explained. "I had someone come up to me [after a show] and she was in tears. She waited until everybody was gone. She was at a place where she needed to hear it.

"Music would have been nice for her, and a message from a 'normal' speaker might have been cool for her," he added. "But the combination of the two – the music opening up the heart and the message being content that goes into the heart absolutely hit her where she needed to hear it.

"She was spilling all of this stuff, and she was basically saying, 'I've known what I need to do. I didn't have the courage to do it. I feel God telling me to do this, and I feel like God put you here today to share this message with me. I'm gonna do it.'"

I wonder what percentage of traditional keynote speeches given by other CEOs and business leaders have garnered that kind of inspiration and commitment to action.

Mike also noted that the universal acceptance of music has allowed him to open doors and gain acceptance from diverse groups of people.

"[In high school] I wasn't solidly a part of any one clique, but was a member of a bunch of them," Mike noted. "It allowed me to have friends whom I'd have never met if it weren't for music, and a fair number are still friends now."

9

Random Thoughts on Music from the Research

Here are some random observations that I have made regarding music and music education based upon my discussions with dozens, if not hundreds, of business leaders, music educators, and musicians during my career.

❑ **Music is spiritual** – Over and over again, people discussed how deeply music affected them, and the term "spiritual" came up repeatedly. Music helps people get in touch with a spiritual side, and helps them feel closer to some sense of a higher power, whether or not they consider themselves religious.

❑ **The Music Mentors** – Teachers in general but especially music mentors have great potential and a tremendous responsibility in shaping the lives of young people. Some of the attributes of great music teachers are cited throughout this book. In general, treating students as individuals and approaching instruction accordingly, being supportive and encouraging regardless of the proficiency of the student, and demonstrating your own passion for music are some of the common traits that separate great music educators.

Many of our culture's great supporters of music receive minimal recognition for their efforts and never get their names on marquees. Music educators often fall into that category. In many cases I mentioned by name the music mentors acknowledged by the participants as having been influential in their lives and careers.

❑ **"You've got to hear my story!"** – When word began to spread regarding the research that I was conducting and the topic of this book, it was amazing how eager people were to lend their stories. CEOs and business leaders with incredible responsibilities and time constraints came forward enthusiastically, because they felt so strongly about this topic. One of the things that made me feel as though I was really on to something was the number of people who ended our discussions with the comment, "I'm so glad you're writing about this topic and getting this story out there."

❑ **Music or an instrument as a companion** – Another common theme that came up during these interviews was the concept of music or a musical instrument serving as a companion or friend of the person, perhaps filling some void in their lives. Guitarists sometimes refer to their instrument by name, such as B.B. King's famed Lucille, and many of the music enthusiasts I spoke to echoed those sentiments.

❑ **Life without music** – I asked most of the subjects how their life was different with music as opposed to what it would have been without it. While many of the responses were revealing and insightful, often the response was, "It's hard to say, because music has always been an integral part of me and played such a substantial role in my life." Music is such an integral part of their identity that they simply couldn't conceptualize that hypothetical.

❑ **Standardized testing** – There seems to be a growing frustration that in an era where right-brain or creative thinking, adaptability, and innovation have never been more important, educational institutions are placing a disproportionate reliance on standardized testing to demonstrate results. Once again, it would be unfair to simply blame the educators. After all, we have demanded accountability and they are trying to respond to public demands. But I'm convinced that some form of assessment of creative and innovative thought must be part of the evaluation equation moving forward.

❑ **The Family Piano** – I asked every one of the subjects to recall and reflect on their earliest memories of music. On so many occasions, those thoughts went back to gathering around, listening to a family member play, or tinkering around with the family piano. I've come to believe that you can change lives with 88 keys.

❑ **The Beatles are the Standard** – The first ten albums that I bought as a kid were Beatles albums. I can remember saving up my change until I had three or four dollars and riding my bike to the department or record store and trying to decide which one I wanted to buy next. Because I interviewed a healthy number of "Baby Boomers," I suspected that the Beatles would be a recurring topic when it came to the musical influences of the participants. It was interesting that even when I spoke to younger people who had influences like Radiohead and Nirvana, they still cited listening to their parents' Beatles albums as defining moments. What a musical legacy.

❑ **Music in "Life's Top Five"** – When the topic of music education funding comes up, I keep thinking back to Neil Moore's assertion that focus groups consistently rank music as one of the top five most important things in their lives. Astounding. How do you replace that in the curriculum?

❑ **Once a Musician...** – People inspired by and significantly impacted by music can move on to other pursuits, but you can't extract the musician from them. Music continues to be their defining characteristic in terms of their own sense of identity. Repeatedly, people who had achieved a tremendous degree of success by any standard told me that they still consider themselves first and foremost musicians.

10

Where Do We Go From Here?

Perhaps one approach to the preservation of the arts is greater integration into what have been considered core subject areas. The use of mind-mapping has become more widely accepted in business as a means of using the art of "doodling" as a vehicle for generating ideas. The theory is that using the parts of the brain that are triggered when someone is drawing is more conducive to creative thought than trying to organize thoughts into outline form, which taps into the logical side of the brain. Think again about the enduring success of the *Schoolhouse Rock* series that we spoke of previously. The concept of integrating music as a learning tool across other areas of the curriculum is an area that deserves greater exploration.

I have used music as an ice-breaker and to facilitate team-building in my own business workshops and training sessions. And I am certainly not alone in that regard. John Hollwitz at Fordham University discussed with me a jazz improvisation exercise that they conduct as part of an orientation session for their incoming M.B.A. class. I have witnessed Dr. Michael Gold's *Jazz Impact* workshop that we discussed previously presented at the M.B.A. class orientation of Loyola University of New Orleans with similar results. Administrators of those programs believe that facilitating music exercises as a team-building tool achieves greater results than those that could have been achieved using other methods.

Yet there's no substitute for music education in its pure form.

Many non-profit organizations are attempting to fill the gap. Yet the greatest opportunity to touch the lives of large numbers of children through music lies in our education system.

No Child Left Behind?

According to a series of reports by the Center on Education Policy that tracks the implementation of the No Child Left Behind Act (which became law in 2002) entitled *From the Capital to the Classroom,* 62 percent of elementary school districts reported increasing time for English and/or math since the 2001-02 school year by an average increase of 42 percent. At the same time, 44 percent of elementary school districts reported cutting time from one or more other subjects including science, social studies, art and music, physical education, lunch, and recess by an average of about 30 minutes per day.

"What gets tested gets taught," said Jack Jennings, CEP's president and CEO. "Because so much is riding on reading and math, included on state tests, many schools have cut back time on other important areas, which means that some students are not receiving a broad curriculum."

The report also notes that these changes are more prevalent in districts that are home to struggling schools. One recommendation from the report is to "include measures of knowledge and skills in art and music as one of the multiple measures used for NCLB accountability."[7]

And the irony is that throughout my research, I consistently heard very successful people say that music kept them engaged in the school experience where they might have become disenchanted with the notion otherwise. There are talented students all

---

[7] Center on Education Policy. (2007). *Choices, Changes, and Challenges: Curriculum and Instruction in the NCLB Era,* a report in the series *From the Capital to the Classroom: Year 5 of the No Child Left Behind Act.* Washington, DC: Jennifer McMurrer.

over school campuses, and many of those children don't respond well to traditional assessment methods or don't feel part of the mainstream. Sometimes tutoring and remedial course offerings are not enough to keep children on the bus. We need to find a motivating reason for them to want to come along for the ride.

In short, music education *is* a no child left behind program.

From the outside looking in, it would be presumptuous of me to tell educators how to run their schools. During my career, I've never had a school principal tell me how to sell environmental consulting and engineering services or material handling equipment.

It does seem to me that the very well-intended accountability motives that have driven the demand for standardized testing have led us to a more narrow approach to education. As discussed at length previously, these changes come in an era where the need for well-rounded and diversified students has never been greater. Perhaps the information contained herein will help us all to take a step back and reassess the current approach before we are too far along this educational evolutionary path.

What I do know for certain is that the 32 professionals and one author who gave their time, energy, and insights to compile these profiles believe strongly that music education was a defining element in the composition of their success.

I offer educators, business leaders, and advocates of music education the benefit of our collective thoughts and experience.

Play on.

ABOUT THE AUTHOR

Craig Cortello, the "Business Musician," is a sought-after speaker/entertainer for corporate, association, and academic gatherings. His presentations regarding the universal lessons of music and enhancing creativity in the workplace are interspersed with his own musical performance, creating an engaging, memorable, and enlightening encounter.

In business, Craig is a 20 year veteran of manufacturing, engineering, and consulting firms, primarily in sales and sales management roles. He most recently served as National Sales Manager of Trinity Consultants, an environmental consulting firm with 28 offices in the U.S. and China. His articles on business creativity have appeared in various publications including *Industrial Engineering* and *Convention Forum* magazines.

In music, Craig is a contributing music writer to *Where Y'at* magazine and *AllAboutJazz.com*, having had the pleasure of interviewing such New Orleans music icons as Pete Fountain, Ellis Marsalis, Jr., Marva Wright, and Henry Butler. He is also a 30 year veteran of the guitar, a self-taught pianist, and a composer. His original composition "New Orleans is the One I Love" served as the title song for the 2007 musical cabaret that served as a fundraiser for Hurricane Katrina first responders who were called to duty despite suffering from the adverse affects of the storm.

He serves as a board member of the National Speakers Association New Orleans Chapter and of the Metairie Sunrise Rotary Club.

He holds a Bachelor of Science degree in Industrial Technology from Southeastern Louisiana University. Craig is a native of the New Orleans metropolitan area where he lives with his wife of 15 years, Kim and his son Michael.

For speaking, training, and book lecture appearances or for more information, visit www.BusinessMusician.com or call 504.304.7167.